What about Threshold Bible Study

"With lucidity and creativity, Stephen Binz offers today's believing communities a rich and accessible treasury of biblical scholarship. The series' brilliance lies in its simplicity of presentation complemented by critical depth of thought and reflective insight."
■ **CAROL J. DEMPSEY, OP**, *Professor of Theology, University of Portland, OR*

"Small groups where men and women of faith can gather to reflect and support each other are essential for the New Evangelization. Stephen Binz has a proven record of supplying excellent resource material to help these groups break open the Scriptures and be nourished and renewed by the living word of God. I commend him for continuing to provide this important service with the *Threshold Bible Study* series."
■ **ARCHBISHOP PAUL-ANDRE DUROCHER**, *Archbishop of Gatineau, Quebec*

"The Church has called Scripture a 'font' and 'wellspring' for the spiritual life. *Threshold Bible Study* is one of the best sources for tapping into the biblical font. *Threshold Bible Study* offers you an encounter with the word that will make your heart come alive."
■ **TIM GRAY**, *President of the Augustine Institute, Denver*

"*Threshold Bible Study* offers solid scholarship and spiritual depth. It can be counted on for lively individual study and prayer, even while it offers spiritual riches to deepen communal conversation and reflection among the people of God."
■ **SCOTT HAHN**, *Founder and President, St. Paul Center for Biblical Theology*

"Stephen Binz provides the Church with a tremendous gift and resource in the *Threshold Bible Study*. This great series invites readers into the world of Scripture with insight, wisdom, and accessibility. This series will help you fall in love with the word of God!"
■ **DANIEL P. HORAN, OFM**, *Catholic Theological Union, Chicago*

"Stephen J. Binz has a unique talent for helping ordinary folks engage the Bible with deep understanding. Graduates of the Hartford Catholic Biblical School are using his *Threshold Bible Study* throughout Connecticut to bring Scripture more fully into the lives of God's people."
■ **B.J. DALY HORELL**, *Director, Catholic Biblical School, Archdiocese of Hartford*

"*Threshold Bible Study* is by far the best series of short Bible study books available today. I recommend them to all the leaders I help train in the Catholic Bible Institutes of several dioceses. Kudos to Stephen Binz for writing books that are ideal for small-group or individual use."
■ **Felix Just, SJ**, *Loyola Marymount University, Los Angeles*

"Stephen Binz's *Threshold Bible Study* series gives adults of all ages a very accessible way to 'open wide the Scriptures' as *Dei Verbum* urged. Encountering the word of God together in study groups will allow participants to deepen their faith and encounter their Savior Jesus."
■ **Archbishop Joseph E. Kurtz**, *Archbishop of Louisville*

"Though the distance many feel between the word of God and their everyday lives can be overwhelming, it need not be so. *Threshold Bible Study* is a fine blend of the best of biblical scholarship and a realistic sensitivity to the spiritual journey of the believing Christian. I recommend it highly."
■ **Francis J. Moloney, SDB**, *Professor, Catholic University of Australia*

"*Threshold Bible Study* is a refreshing approach to enable participants to ponder the Scriptures more deeply. This series provides a practical way for faithful people to get to know the Bible better and to enjoy the fruits of biblical prayer."
■ **Irene Nowell, OSB**, *Mount St. Scholastica, Atchison, KS*

"*Threshold Bible Study* is appropriately named, for its commentary and study questions bring people to the threshold of the text and invite them in. The questions guide but do not dominate. Stephen Binz's work stands in the tradition of the biblical renewal movement and brings it back to life."
■ **Kathleen M. O'Connor**, *Professor Emerita, Columbia Theological Seminary*

"Stephen J. Binz is a consistently outstanding Catholic educator and communicator whose books on the study and application of Scripture have thoroughly enriched my Christian understanding. In our fast-moving, often confusing times, his ability to help us examine and comprehend the truth through all the noise is especially needed and valuable."
■ **Elizabeth Scalia**, *writer and speaker, editor at Aleteia, blogger as The Anchoress*

"*Threshold Bible Study* helpfully introduces the lay reader to the life-enhancing process of *lectio divina*, individually or in a group. This series leads the reader from Bible study to personal prayer, community involvement, and active Christian commitment in the world."
■ **Sandra M. Schneiders**, *Professor, Jesuit School of Theology at Santa Clara University*

"Stephen Binz has created an essential resource for the new evangelization rooted in the discipleship process that helps participants to unpack the treasures of the Scriptures in an engaging and accessible manner. *Threshold Bible Study* connects faith learning to faithful living, leading one to a deeper relationship with Christ and his body, the Church."
■ **Julianne Stanz**, *Director of New Evangelization, Diocese of Green Bay*

New Covenant Worship

Hebrews

Stephen J. Binz

twentythirdpublications.com

TWENTY-THIRD PUBLICATIONS
One Montauk Avenue, Suite 200
New London, CT 06320
(860) 437-3012 or (800) 321-0411
www.twentythirdpublications.com

Copyright ©2022 Stephen J. Binz. All rights reserved. No part of this publication may be reproduced in any manner without prior written permission of the publisher. Write to the Permissions Editor.

The Scripture passages contained herein are from the *New Revised Standard Version Bible*, Catholic edition. Copyright ©1989, by the Division of Christian Education of the National Council of the Churches of Christ in the U.S.A. All rights reserved.

ISBN: 978-1-62785-677-5
Printed in the U.S.A.

Contents

HOW TO USE *THRESHOLD BIBLE STUDY* vii
   Suggestions for individual study ix
   Suggestions for group study x

INTRODUCTION 1
   Suggestions for Facilitators, Group Session 1 11

LESSONS 1–6
   1. God Has Spoken through His Son *(Hebrews 1:1–4)* 12
   2. The Majesty of God's Son *(Hebrews 1:5–14)* 15
   3. The Urgency of the Son's Revelation *(Hebrews 2:1–4)* 19
   4. The Suffering and Exaltation of Jesus *(Hebrews 2:5–18)* 22
   5. The Faithful Son Placed over the House of God *(Hebrews 3:1–6)* 26
   6. Be Faithful as Partners of Christ *(Hebrews 3:7–19)* 29
      Suggestions for Facilitators, Group Session 2 32

LESSONS 7–12
   7. The Rest that God Promised *(Hebrews 4:1–11)* 33
   8. Jesus Is the Great High Priest *(Hebrews 4:12–16)* 36
   9. The High Priest in the Old and New Covenants *(Hebrews 5:1–10)* 39
   10. Moving from Infancy to Maturity in Faith *(Hebrews 5:11—6:3)* 43
   11. Remain Faithful until Hope Is Fulfilled *(Hebrews 6:4–12)* 46
   12. Hope in God's Steadfast Promises *(Hebrews 6:13–20)* 49
      Suggestions for Facilitators, Group Session 3 52

LESSONS 13–18

13.	Melchizedek, the Priest and King *(Hebrews 7:1–10)*	53
14.	A New High Priest Resembling Melchizedek *(Hebrews 7:11–28)*	57
15.	High Priest of the New Covenant *(Hebrews 8:1–6)*	61
16.	The New Covenant for God's People *(Hebrews 8:7–13)*	64
17.	The Completeness of Christ's Sacrifice *(Hebrews 9:1–14)*	68
18.	The New Covenant Sacrifice *(Hebrews 9:15–28)*	72
	Suggestions for Facilitators, Group Session 4	76

LESSONS 19–24

19.	The Singular Self-Offering of Christ *(Hebrews 10:1–10)*	77
20.	The Enthroned High Priest *(Hebrews 10:11–18)*	80
21.	Call to Worship, Faith, and Perseverance *(Hebrews 10:19–39)*	83
22.	Examples of Faith *(Hebrews 11:1–7)*	87
23.	Israel's Ancestors Lived by Faith *(Hebrews 11:8–22)*	90
24.	All Were Waiting for God's Promise *(Hebrews 11:23–40)*	94
	Suggestions for Facilitators, Group Session 5	98

LESSONS 25–30

25.	Jesus the Pioneer and Perfecter of Faith *(Hebrews 12:1–11)*	99
26.	Let No One Fail to Obtain God's Grace *(Hebrews 12:12–17)*	103
27.	The Earthly Sinai and the Heavenly Zion *(Hebrews 12:18–29)*	106
28.	Encouragement to Live a Transformed Life *(Hebrews 13:1–8)*	110
29.	Offering Sacrifice to God through Christ *(Hebrews 13:9–16)*	114
30.	Final Blessing and Postscript *(Hebrews 13:17–25)*	118
	Suggestions for Facilitators, Group Session 6	122

How to Use
Threshold Bible Study

Threshold Bible Study is a dynamic, informative, inspiring, and life-changing series that helps you learn about Scripture in a whole new way. Each book will help you explore new dimensions of faith and discover deeper insights for your life as a disciple of Jesus.

The threshold is a place of transition. The threshold of God's word invites you to enter that place where God's truth, goodness, and beauty can shine into your life and fill your mind and heart. Through the Holy Spirit, the threshold becomes holy ground, sacred space, and graced time. God can teach you best at the threshold, because God opens your life to his word and fills you with the Spirit of truth.

With *Threshold Bible Study*, each topic or book of the Bible is approached in a thematic way. You will understand and reflect on the biblical texts through overarching themes derived from biblical theology. Through this method, the study of Scripture will impact your life in a unique way and transform you from within.

These books are designed for maximum flexibility. Each study is presented in a workbook format, with sections for reading, reflecting, writing, discussing, and praying. Each *Threshold* book contains thirty lessons, which you can use for your daily study over the course of a month or which can be divided into six lessons per week, providing a group study of six weekly sessions. These studies are ideal for Bible study groups, small Christian communities, adult faith formation, student groups, Sunday school, neighborhood groups, and family reading, as well as for individual learning.

The commentary that follows each biblical passage launches your reflection on that passage and helps you begin to see its significance within the context of your contemporary experience. The questions following the commentary challenge you to understand the passage more fully and apply it to your own life. Space for writing after each question is ideal for personal study and also allows group participants to prepare in advance for the weekly discussion. The prayer helps conclude your study each day by integrating your learning into your relationship with God.

The method of *Threshold Bible Study* is rooted in the ancient tradition of *lectio divina*, whereby studying the Bible becomes a means of deeper intimacy with God and a transformed life. Reading and interpreting the text (*lectio*) is followed by reflective meditation on its message (*meditatio*). This reading and reflecting flows into prayer from the heart (*oratio* and *contemplatio*). In this way, one listens to God through the Scripture and then responds to God in prayer.

This ancient method assures you that Bible study is a matter of both the mind and the heart. It is not just an intellectual exercise to learn more and be able to discuss the Bible with others. It is, more importantly, a transforming experience. Reflecting on God's word, guided by the Holy Spirit, illumines the mind with wisdom and stirs the heart with zeal.

Following the personal Bible study, *Threshold Bible Study* offers ways to extend personal *lectio divina* into a weekly conversation with others. This communal experience will allow participants to enhance their appreciation of the message and build up a spiritual community (*collatio*). The end result will be to increase not only individual faith, but also faithful witness in the context of daily life (*operatio*).

When bringing *Threshold Bible Study* to a church community, try to make every effort to include as many people as possible. Many will want to study on their own; others will want to study with family, a group of friends, or a few work associates; some may want to commit themselves to share insights through a weekly conference call, daily text messaging, or an online social network; and others will want to gather weekly in established small groups.

By encouraging *Threshold Bible Study* and respecting the many ways people desire to make Bible study a regular part of their lives, you will widen the number of people in your church community who study the Bible regularly in whatever way they are able in their busy lives. Simply sign up people at the Sunday services and order bulk quantities for your church. Encourage people to follow the daily study as faithfully as they can. This encouragement can be through Sunday announcements, notices in parish publications, support on the church website, and other creative invitations and motivations.

Through the spiritual disciplines of Scripture reading, study, reflection, conversation, and prayer, *Threshold Bible Study* will help you experience God's grace more abundantly and root your life more deeply in Christ. The risen Jesus said: "Listen! I am standing at the door, knocking; if you hear my voice and open the door, I will come in to you and eat with you, and you with me" (Rev 3:20). Listen to the word of God, open the door, and cross the threshold to an unimaginable dwelling with God!

SUGGESTIONS FOR INDIVIDUAL STUDY

- Make your Bible reading a time of prayer. Ask for God's guidance as you read the Scriptures.

- Try to study daily, or as often as possible according to the circumstances of your life.

- Read the Bible passage carefully, trying to understand both its meaning and its personal application as you read. Some persons find it helpful to read the passage aloud.

- Read the passage in another Bible translation. Each version adds to your understanding of the original text.

- Allow the commentary to help you comprehend and apply the scriptural text. The commentary is only a beginning, not the last word, on the meaning of the passage.

- After reflecting on each question, write out your responses. The very act of writing will help you clarify your thoughts, bring new insights, and amplify your understanding.

- As you reflect on your answers, think about how you can live God's word in the context of your daily life.

- Conclude each daily lesson by reading the prayer and continuing with your own prayer from the heart.

- Make sure your reflections and prayers are matters of both the mind and the heart. A true encounter with God's word is always a transforming experience.

- Choose a word or a phrase from the lesson to carry with you throughout the day as a reminder of your encounter with God's life-changing word.

- For additional insights and affirmation, share your learning experience with at least one other person whom you trust. The ideal way to share learning is in a small group that meets regularly.

SUGGESTIONS FOR GROUP STUDY

- Meet regularly; weekly is ideal. Try to be on time and make attendance a high priority for the sake of the group. The average group meets for about an hour.

- Open each session with a prepared prayer, a song, or a reflection. Find some appropriate way to bring the group from the workaday world into a sacred time of graced sharing.

- If you have not been together before, name tags are very helpful as a group begins to become acquainted with the other group members.

- Spend the first session getting acquainted with one another, reading the Introduction aloud, and discussing the questions that follow.

- Appoint a group facilitator to provide guidance to the discussion. The role of facilitator may rotate among members each week. The facilitator simply keeps the discussion on track; each person shares responsibility for the group. There is no need for the facilitator to be a trained teacher.

- Try to study the six lessons on your own during the week. When you have done your own reflection and written your own answers, you will be better prepared to discuss the six scriptural lessons with the group. If you have not had an opportunity to study the passages during the week, meet with the group anyway to share support and insights.

- Participate in the discussion as much as you are able, offering your thoughts, insights, feelings, and decisions. You learn by sharing with others the fruits of your study.

- Be careful not to dominate the discussion. It is important that everyone in the group be offered an equal opportunity to share the results of their work. Try to link what you say to the comments of others so that the group remains on the topic.

- When discussing your own personal thoughts or feelings, use "I" language. Be as personal and honest as appropriate and be very cautious about giving advice to others.

- Listen attentively to the other members of the group so as to learn from their insights. The words of the Bible affect each person in a different way, so a group provides a wealth of understanding for each member.

- Don't fear silence. Silence in a group is as important as silence in personal study. It allows individuals time to listen to the voice of God's Spirit and the opportunity to form their thoughts before they speak.

- Solicit several responses for each question. The thoughts of different people will build on the answers of others and will lead to deeper insights for all.

- Don't fear controversy. Differences of opinions are a sign of a healthy and honest group. If you cannot resolve an issue, continue on, agreeing to disagree. There is probably some truth in each viewpoint.

- Discuss the questions that seem most important for the group. There is no need to cover all the questions in the group session.

- Realize that some questions about the Bible cannot be resolved, even by experts. Don't get stuck on some issue for which there are no clear answers.

- Whatever is said in the group is said in confidence and should be regarded as such.

- Pray as a group in whatever way feels comfortable. Pray for the members of your group throughout the week.

Schedule for Group Study

Session 1: Introduction   Date: _____

Session 2: Lessons 1–6   Date: _____

Session 3: Lessons 7–12   Date: _____

Session 4: Lessons 13–18   Date: _____

Session 5: Lessons 19–24   Date: _____

Session 6: Lessons 25–30   Date: _____

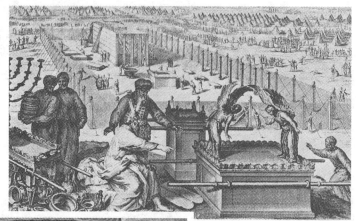

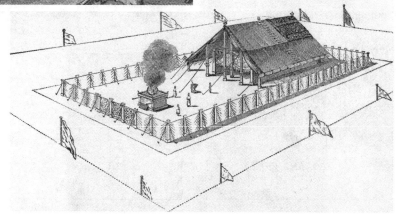

INTRODUCTION SESSION 1

> "The days are surely coming, says the Lord, when I will establish a new covenant with the house of Israel and with the house of Judah." HEBREWS 8:8

New Covenant Worship

As we begin to study Hebrews, we ought to imagine ourselves not at a desk reading a book or a letter but with a congregation listening to an eloquent preacher. Although we don't know the identity of the author—speculation has centered from the earliest days on Paul, Barnabas, Apollos, and Priscilla—the homilist is helping the assembly understand a longing that is at the heart of every human being: the desire to draw near to God in worship. All religion, at its root, is an expression of this yearning to approach and encounter God.

Don't we often have the feeling that everything in this world is incomplete? We are continually confronted with the limitations of our human existence. Wouldn't it be true to say that the realities of this life fail to satisfy our deepest longings? No matter how much we have, we are never really satisfied. Possessions, power, and pleasure fail to satisfy the inmost desires of the human heart. Even our experiences of genuine love—the joining of spouses and the truest human friendships—leave a longing for an encounter that is even fuller and more lasting.

Hebrews teaches that Jesus Christ is the one who can take us into the presence of God and fulfill our truest desires. In Christian worship we glimpse the completion of human longing. There we realize that our anxious yearnings can be satisfied. Jesus is the one who is able to remove the barriers between this world and heaven, between our sinful humanity and God's all-holy presence. Jesus is the bridge, the perfect mediator between us and God.

Although the author of Hebrews is anonymous, we can be certain of two characteristics. First, the author knew the Greek language well. The work contains some of the most polished language in the New Testament. Second, the author knew the Hebrew Scriptures thoroughly. The work contains at least thirty-six quotations and countless references from the Old Testament. Jewish history, traditions, feasts, and heroes form the foundation on which the whole homily is constructed. So Hebrews expresses the truth of Christian worship within the overlapping contexts of Greek philosophy and Jewish tradition.

The Greek style and ideas make the reading challenging, with every passage packed with meaning. The Greek philosopher Plato and his many disciples taught that the present reality in which we live is only a shadow of the real world. This world is only an imperfect reflection of the eternal domain. Every person, then, seeks to get beyond the specters and imperfections of this world in order to experience what is real, eternal, and true. This is exactly what Hebrews claims Jesus Christ enables us to do. In Jesus Christ, the divine world (of the fullest and truest reality) and the earthly world (of transient, shadowy reality) are joined.

The Jewish mindset challenges us to understand the Old Testament background in order to comprehend the truth about Jesus and the consequences of his life for our own. The whole system of covenant, priesthood, and sacrifice brings the people of Israel near to God in worship. The covenant, the expression of their relationship with God, is rooted in God's promises and Israel's obedient response to God's will. Yet, as the prophets testify, God's people continually broke the covenant, creating barriers to the divine presence through their sin. The priesthood mediates between the people and God, offering gifts from the people to God and seeking pardon from God. Sacrifices are offered daily in the temple of Jerusalem to gain access to divine life, and the blood of sacrificed animals is poured out in an attempt to atone for sins. Hebrews makes the bold claim that Jesus Christ is the fulfillment of all of Israel's institutions for worshiping God. He is the new covenant, forming a renewed relationship, enabling us to participate in God's life. In his complete self-giving on the cross, offered in love unto death, he has become the perfect priest and the perfect sacrifice. The barrier erected by sin has been broken, and we can draw near to God in the perfect worship of the new covenant.

Reflection and discussion
- How has my human longing for fulfillment led me to worship God?

- How does worshiping through Jesus Christ make worship complete?

Sacrifice at the Heart of Worshiping God
Sacrifice was practiced by almost all ancient religions. In Israel, sacrifice took its own unique form through the centuries but with many parallels to the sacrificial practices of its neighbors in the ancient Middle East. The Bible depicts sacrifice as an element of human worship of God from the beginnings of humanity, as illustrated in the sacrifices of Cain and Abel (Gen 4:3–4). As in all ancient sacrificial worship, the victim becomes a link between the world of those offering sacrifice and the transcendent realm: its body belongs to the physical world and its life belongs to the spiritual domain. The essential purpose of sacrifice is to maintain or reestablish unity with the divine world.

A significant part of Israel's Torah describes its sacrifices. The altar was a focal point for Israel's worship, and priests offered sacrifices on behalf of the whole community of Israel or on behalf of individuals who brought animals or other fruits of their lives for sacrifice. Leviticus describes several types of animal sacrifices, each differing in the purpose and details of its offering. The burnt offering (Lev 1) consisted of a sacrifice to God in which an unblemished animal was ritually slaughtered, its blood dashed at the base of the altar, and its flesh was consumed in the fire on the altar. The sacrifice of well-being or peace (Lev 3) was offered on the altar, and its meat was then shared by the worshipers in a joyful meal.

For the sin offering (Lev 4), the person presenting the sacrifice laid his hand on the head of the animal victim in order to identify with it. The pouring out of the blood, which represents the life of the sacrificed victim, represents the self-offering of the person to God. The blood is sprinkled in the sanctuary, smeared on the horned corners of the altar, or poured out at the base of the altar to purge the effects of sin from the people, creating atonement with God.

Sacrifices were offered every day in the temple, consisting of burnt offerings of one lamb in the morning and one in the evening (Exod 29:38–39). The Torah describes the various types of sacrifices that were to be offered on each of the feasts of Israel: the new moon, Passover, Pentecost, New Year's Day, the Day of Atonement, and the Feast of Booths (Num 28—29). In addition, the firstborn son of human families, the first offspring of animals, and the firstfruits of each year's crop were regarded as belonging to God. The firstborn of clean animals had to be sacrificed to God; likewise, the firstfruits of the fields were offered to God. The firstborn sons, however, were not sacrificed; an animal was sacrificed as a substitute for them.

When we imagine the rituals of ancient Israel—animals slaughtered, the smoke of sacrifice rising every day from the altar, specific offerings required for every time and season—we may be tempted to think of Israel's religion as overly external and ritualistic. Yet we must remember that the sacrificial laws are rooted in the personal, covenantal bond between God and Israel. Sacrifice is an expression of that primary relationship, either deepening or renewing that bond. While the elements of sacrifice are symbolic—the animal, the blood, the altar, the burning, the eating—nevertheless, according to the faith of Israel, the ritual elements actually bring about the deepened and renewed bond they symbolize. The covenant between God and Israel presupposes that the underlying disposition beneath the act of sacrifice is a pure heart seeking God. External rituals of sacrifice outwardly express the internal desires within individuals to worship God, repent of sin, and celebrate the covenant.

The prophets and priests of Israel played different roles in the covenantal life of the people, and they were continually in tension because they emphasized different aspects of the covenant bond. The priests were naturally concerned with carrying out the prescribed rituals and thus emphasized the external aspects of sacrifice. The prophets, however, were concerned with the heart. They criticized the status quo in Israel and were continually calling the people to reform and renewal—to return to the heart of the covenant. In matters of sacrifice, the prophets often challenged the ritualistic and external aspects and emphasized the everyday life of the people in relationship to God and their neighbors. They taught that external sacrifice could never substitute for justice and compassion and that leading a just life was necessary for offering sacrifice. Genuine worship was a matter of the heart as well as external actions.

In the writings of Micah the people ask how they are to worship God, and they propose various forms of sacrifice: holocausts, thousands of rams, offering the firstborn. The prophet replies that the people have already been told what God requires: "to do justice, and to love kindness, and to walk humbly with your God" (Mic 6:6–8). The prophecies of Amos might sound like a rejection of ritual but are actually highly charged rhetoric proclaiming that exterior rites must be accompanied by right conduct and the practice of justice. The prophet speaks the word of the Lord: "Even though you offer me your burnt offerings and grain offerings, I will not accept them, and the offerings of well-being of your fatted animals I will not look upon....But let justice roll down like waters, and righteousness like an ever-flowing stream" (Amos 5:22–24). Hosea expresses what must be at the heart of ritual offerings: "For I desire steadfast love and not sacrifice, the knowledge of God rather than burnt offerings" (Hos 6:6).

Reflection and discussion
- Why was animal sacrifice such a universal form of worship in the ancient world?

- Why are both external ritual and internal disposition necessary for genuine worship?

New Covenant Sacrifice

Jesus was firmly rooted in the tradition of Israel, and the gospels narrate his journeys to Jerusalem to participate in the sacrificial feasts. Yet he enhanced the teaching of the prophets by insisting that his followers seek reconciliation over any offense before bringing a sacrifice to be offered in the temple (Matt 5:23). He situates their ritual actions within the context of obeying the greatest commandments. Loving God and neighbor, he proclaimed, "is much more important than all whole burnt offerings and sacrifices" (Mark 12:33).

The passion narratives of the four gospels demonstrate how the apostolic church grew to understand that Jesus' death was a sacrificial offering. Turning to the Suffering Servant texts of the prophet Isaiah, they understood that the innocent death of God's Servant on behalf of the many (i.e., the nations of the world) was a type of sin offering: "He poured out himself to death, and was numbered with the transgressors; yet he bore the sin of many, and made intercession for the transgressors" (Isa 53:12). The words of Jesus in Mark's gospel refer to this ancient passage of Isaiah: "The Son of Man came not to be served but to serve, and to give his life a ransom for many" (Mark 10:45). Likewise, in Luke's gospel Jesus states that Isaiah 53 was written about himself and that in his passion the text is coming to its fulfillment (Luke 22:37). In these ways, the ancient texts open the way for interpreting the self-offering of Jesus as a completion of the old covenant sacrifices and their atoning effect.

The Last Supper accounts emphasize the sacrificial nature of Christ's death by situating the Passion in the context of the Passover, with its sacrifice of the lambs in the temple and the shedding of blood that accompanied it. The words of Jesus, "This is my blood of the covenant, which is poured out for many" (Mark 14:24), allude to the inauguration of the ancient covenant on Sinai with its sacrifice, the shedding of blood, and its sacrificial meal (Exod 24:1–11). In the account of Matthew, the words "for the forgiveness of sins" (Matt 26:28) are added in order to make clear the purpose of Christ's death as a sin offering. Every time the Eucharist is celebrated, the sacrifice of Christ on the cross becomes a present reality for us.

In the earliest New Testament writings, Paul expresses the church's understanding that the passion and death of Christ is a sacrificial offering: "Our paschal lamb, Christ, has been sacrificed" (1 Cor 5:7). He is the new lamb of the Passover feast, given up for us and memorialized in every Eucharist: "For as often as you eat this bread and drink the cup, you proclaim the Lord's death until he comes" (1 Cor 11:26). In writing to the Ephesians, Paul states that Christ's offering was a sacrifice given out of love for us: "Christ loved us and gave himself up for us, a fragrant offering and sacrifice to God" (Eph 5:2).

As Jesus enters his ministry in John's gospel, the Baptist declares, "Here is the Lamb of God who takes away the sin of the world!" (John 1:29). This title of Jesus is rooted in both the lamb of the Passover, offered to save God's people (Exod 12), and the Suffering Servant, led like a lamb to be sacrificed as a sin offering (Isa 53:7, 10). Jesus is the Passover Lamb of the new covenant, who died on the cross at the same hour as the lambs were being sacrificed at the temple for the Passover meal (John 19:31). In Revelation, this same Lamb, who was slain in sacrifice, now stands in the midst of the heavenly assembly, still bearing the marks of its sacrificial death (Rev 5:6, 9, 12).

The "blood of the Lamb" makes white the robes of the Christian martyrs as they stand before the heavenly throne (Rev 7:14), and through this blood they have conquered evil and sin (Rev 12:11).

In Hebrews we find the most thorough discussion of the priestly sacrifice of Christ. The homilist presents Jesus as both the priest and the victim, the one who offers the sacrifice and the one who is sacrificed. His death on the cross and his glorification was the one sacrifice that all the many sacrifices of the Old Testament prefigured. The homilist demonstrates that the sacrifices of the old covenant, offered again and again, were only temporary in their effectiveness. But the atoning sacrifice of Christ was offered "once for all," the final sacrifice of God's saving plan in atonement for the sins of the whole world (Heb 9:25–28).

Reflection and discussion
- How does the new covenant sacrifice differ from that of the old covenant?

- What does the phrase "once for all" tell me about the effectiveness and the scope of the self-offering of Christ?

A Priestly People Offering Sacrifice

The saving death and resurrection of Jesus gives a rich new meaning to sacrificial worship. "Through the offering of the body of Jesus Christ once for all" (Heb 10:10) and the sending of the Holy Spirit, the effects of his sacrifice are extended throughout eternity as he is forever interceding for us before the throne of God. So by uniting our lives to Jesus Christ, we not only receive the saving graces of his sacrifice, but we are able to join our whole life to his as a sacrifice to God.

In Christ the whole Christian community becomes a "holy priesthood," a "royal priesthood," united to the priesthood of Christ and offering "spiritual sacrifices acceptable to God through Jesus Christ" (1 Pet 2:5, 9). Everything we do, even the most lowly tasks—our prayers, works, joys, and sufferings—can shine with glory in God's eyes because they are united with the perfect sacrifice of Christ. Paul writes: "I appeal to you…to present your bodies as a living sacrifice, holy and acceptable to God, which is your spiritual worship" (Rom 12:1). What God desires most of all is our hearts united with the heart of Christ. It is that love, overflowing into deeds of loving service, which becomes the living sacrifice that is always pleasing to God.

Hebrews exhorts us: "Through him, then, let us continually offer a sacrifice of praise to God….Do not neglect to do good and to share what you have, for such sacrifices are pleasing to God" (Heb 13:15–16). This expresses what the Christian life is all about: living our lives in union with Christ so that our lives become an offering to God who is worthy of all honor and praise. All the good that we do, all the pain we endure, all the prayers we offer, all the joy of living and loving we experience—our whole lives become an ongoing offering to the Father. Through Christ, with Christ, and in Christ, in the unity of the Holy Spirit, we lift up our lives so that everything we do has eternal meaning and benefit, not only for ourselves but for those we love and indeed for the whole world.

We are similar in so many ways to the original audience of this homily. We seek happiness and fulfillment in ways that fail to satisfy. We long for God but we don't know how to encounter God's presence. We get discouraged; we feel like we've lost the fire. But Hebrews calls us to a deeper reflection on what Christ has done for us so that we will be given renewed faith, vigor, and confidence.

The most important reality expressed in this homily for weary believers is that Jesus continues to act for us. Jesus is alive and active now, interceding for us. "Today" is the time to focus on. Jesus is one with God and one with us. As the homilist proclaims, "Jesus Christ is the same yesterday and today and forever" (13:8). As we share in his life, we enter a new way of existing. In Christ, we have nothing to fear, not even death. So we are free to serve, free to live fully, free to experience all that God wants to share with us.

Reflection and discussion
- How could I more consciously offer my daily life as a sacrifice of praise to God?

- In what way do I hope this study of Hebrews will renew my life?

Prayer
Lord God, you led your inspired writer to offer this message of exhortation to the early Christians. Prepare my mind and heart to study this sacred text so that I will understand more fully the riches of Christ and the grace of the new covenant. Guide my reading and meditation so that it leads me to prayer and witness, so that my life may be a sacrifice of praise to your holy name. Keep me faithful during these weeks to the challenges that your word offers to me.

SUGGESTIONS FOR FACILITATORS, GROUP SESSION 1

1. If the group is meeting for the first time, or if there are newcomers joining the group, it is helpful to provide name tags.

2. Distribute the books to the members of the group.

3. You may want to ask the participants to introduce themselves and tell the group a bit about themselves.

4. Ask one or more of these introductory questions:
   - What drew you to join this group?
   - What is your biggest fear in beginning this Bible study?
   - How is beginning this study like a "threshold" for you?

5. You may want to pray this prayer as a group:
   Come upon us, Holy Spirit, to enlighten and guide us as we begin this study of Hebrews. You inspired the authors of Scripture to reveal your presence throughout the history of salvation. This inspired word has the power to convert our hearts and change our lives. Fill our hearts with desire, trust, and confidence as you shine the light of your truth within us. Motivate us to read the Scriptures and give us a deeper love for God's word each day. Bless us during this session and throughout the coming week with the fire of your love.

6. Read the Introduction aloud, pausing at each question for discussion. Group members may wish to write the insights of the group as each question is discussed. Encourage several members of the group to respond to each question.

7. Don't feel compelled to finish the complete Introduction during the session. It is better to allow sufficient time to talk about the questions raised than to rush to the end. Group members may read any remaining sections on their own after the group meeting.

8. Instruct group members to read the first six lessons on their own during the six days before the next group meeting. They should write out their own answers to the questions as preparation for next week's group discussion.

9. Fill in the date for each group meeting under "Schedule for Group Study."

10. Conclude by praying aloud together the prayer at the end of the Introduction.

LESSON 1 SESSION 2

> **He is the reflection of God's glory and the exact imprint of God's very being, and he sustains all things by his powerful word.** HEBREWS 1:3

God Has Spoken through His Son

HEBREWS 1:1–4 ¹*Long ago God spoke to our ancestors in many and various ways by the prophets,* ²*but in these last days he has spoken to us by a Son, whom he appointed heir of all things, through whom he also created the worlds.* ³*He is the reflection of God's glory and the exact imprint of God's very being, and he sustains all things by his powerful word. When he had made purification for sins, he sat down at the right hand of the Majesty on high,* ⁴*having become as much superior to angels as the name he has inherited is more excellent than theirs.*

The homily begins by affirming what is foundational for the Christian faith: God has spoken. God has not remained silent, hidden in darkness; rather, God has revealed himself to the world, bringing the light of truth to people longing for deliverance and purpose. This divine revelation has been given in two stages: the past and the present, corresponding to the old and new covenants respectively. In ages past, God spoke in a variety of ways through prophets, priests, kings, and sages. God spoke in storm and thunder to Moses, and in a small whisper to Elijah. Yet all these divine acts and varying modes of revelation did not add up to the fullness of what God had to say. "But in these last days," the time described in the prophets as the age of fulfillment, God has spoken through his Son, Jesus Christ. In him, God has now spoken his climactic, definitive, decisive word. In the past, God's revelation had been a series of progressive promises, but now, God has completed the plan, fulfilling all promises in the Son. Through the long biblical story, we can now see how wisely and carefully God had been preparing his people for the final gift of Jesus Christ.

Although God had been speaking in the past through servants, messengers, prophets, visions, and oracles, God's self-revelation through the Son is the fullest he can offer the world. The preacher now expresses a series of qualities, spelling out several distinct aspects of the Son's nature and saving work, showing why he is God's final and most complete self-communication.

First, the Son has been appointed by God as "heir of all things" (verse 2). This inheritance includes not only the bequest God gave to Abraham and his descendants but also what God promised to his Son in Psalm 2: "I will make the nations your heritage, and the ends of the earth your possession" (Ps 2:7–8). Yet the Son is also the one through whom God "created the worlds" and the one who "sustains all things by his powerful word" (verses 2–3). The truth that God brought the whole universe of space and time into being through the agency of his Son is confirmed by other writers: "All things came into being through him, and without him not one thing came into being" (John 1:3) and "All things have been created through him and for him" (Col 1:16). But the creative word that calls the universe into being requires also a sustaining utterance by which it is maintained in being. So the Son, who was with God from the beginning of creation, is with God now in sustaining all things in existence, and in the future he will inherit the universe in its perfection.

As "the reflection of God's glory" (verse 3), the Son is the radiance that shines forth from the inner being of God into the world. He is God made visible, shining God's light into the hearts of God's people. As "the exact imprint of God's very being," the Son is the precise representation and embodiment of the Father. Like a stamp or seal makes an impression on a soft surface, what God essentially is, is made manifest in Christ. To encounter Jesus is to know in the fullest sense what God is like.

The preacher moves from describing the eternal and cosmic being of the Son to his personal relationship with humanity as our sacrifice and high priest. In Christ's saving death and resurrection, he has "made purification for sins."

The one through whom and for whom the universe was created is the one who has saved us from the defilement of sin by freely offering his life to the Father on our behalf. Now he is seated "at the right hand of the Majesty on high," an image that denotes the position of highest honor and authority in the kingdom. At his Passion, Jesus applied Psalm 110 to himself in which God says to his anointed one, "Sit at my right hand" (Ps 110:1; Luke 22:69). He is now exalted in glory and intercedes for us eternally before the Father, holding a position and a name that is far superior to even God's highest creatures, the angels.

Reflection and discussion

- What are some of the ways I have experienced God "speaking" to me?

- How attentively do I listen to God's voice as it comes to me in the Scriptures?

- Which of the Son's unique qualities listed in these verses is most helpful to me in understanding why he is God's most complete revelation?

Prayer

Creator God, you have spoken throughout the history of salvation in partial and various ways. Speak to me now through your Son, Jesus Christ. Help me to marvel at how he who sustains the entire universe also forgives my sins and those of each person in the world.

LESSON 2  SESSION 2

> "Your throne, O God, is forever and ever, and the righteous scepter is the scepter of your kingdom."
> HEBREWS 1:8

The Majesty of God's Son

HEBREWS 1:5–14

⁵*For to which of the angels did God ever say,*
  "You are my Son;
    today I have begotten you"?
Or again,
  "I will be his Father,
    and he will be my Son"?
⁶*And again, when he brings the firstborn into the world, he says,*
  "Let all God's angels worship him."
⁷*Of the angels he says,*
  "He makes his angels winds,
    and his servants flames of fire."
⁸*But of the Son he says,*
  "Your throne, O God, is forever and ever,
    and the righteous scepter is the scepter of your kingdom.
⁹*You have loved righteousness and hated wickedness;*
therefore God, your God, has anointed you
  with the oil of gladness beyond your companions."
¹⁰*And,*
  "In the beginning, Lord, you founded the earth,
    and the heavens are the work of your hands;

> ¹¹*they will perish, but you remain;*
>   *they will all wear out like clothing;*
> ¹²*like a cloak you will roll them up,*
>   *and like clothing they will be changed.*
> *But you are the same,*
>   *and your years will never end."*
> ¹³*But to which of the angels has he ever said,*
>   *"Sit at my right hand*
>   *until I make your enemies a footstool for your feet"?*
> ¹⁴*Are not all angels spirits in the divine service, sent to serve for the sake of those who are to inherit salvation?*

The weary Christians who listened to this homily needed reassurance to believe that the crucified Jesus was also the exalted Lord. The preacher has made the claim that Christ is far superior to the angels and is the eternal Son of the Father. Now, he links together a chain of quotations from the old covenant Scriptures to support these assertions of Christ's divinity.

The first quotation, "You are my Son; today I have begotten you," was never addressed by God to an angel. It was originally spoken about the king from the line of David (Ps 2:7), and in later centuries about the Messiah who would come in the age of fulfillment. The early Christians interpreted these words to refer to Jesus Christ, the eternally begotten Son of God. The next citation, "I will be his Father, and he will be my Son," comes from God's promises about the future descendant of David whose royal throne will last forever (2 Sam 7:13–14), a promise fulfilled in Christ. The third quote, "Let all God's angels worship him" (see Ps 97:7, Greek version), refers to the worship that is due to Christ from angels and all other creatures because he is God's "firstborn." In the old covenant, the firstborn son received the father's blessing and inheritance. Jesus Christ is God's "firstborn," the Son who existed before all creation and is thus worthy of all praise and worship by the angels in the divine liturgy of heaven.

As important as the angels are in God's administration of the universe, their role is far inferior to the supremacy given to the Son. The next quotations deepen the contrast between the angels, who are creatures (verse 7), and the Son, who is divine (verses 8–12). God's angels are manifested in the world like the natural elements of wind and fire: "He makes his angels winds, and his servants flames of fire" (Ps 104:4, Greek version). Yet, when compared to the next verses about the eternal power and majesty of the Son, the angels seem to be fleeting like the wind and flickering like fire.

In contrast, the preacher quotes a royal psalm describing the wedding of the anointed king (Ps 45:6–7). As the resurrected Messiah and Lord, Jesus Christ most fully fits this royal portrait. His throne is eternal and he holds the scepter of God's everlasting kingdom. As the divine Messiah, he loves righteousness and hates wickedness and may be properly addressed as "God" (verses 8–9). The preacher continues by citing Psalm 102:25–27, applying the description of God to Jesus Christ. He is the Lord who established the heavens and the earth (verse 10). While all created things will pass away, like worn-out clothing, the Son of God is unchanging and eternal (verses 11–12).

The chain of quotations is concluded with the same rhetorical question with which it began: "To which of the angels did God ever say…?" (verses 5, 13). The preacher inserts a final text from the psalms: "Sit at my right hand until I make your enemies a footstool for your feet" (Ps 110:1). No such promise was ever made to an angel, but it was made to the Messiah and is fulfilled in Jesus, who reigns at the Father's right hand, the place of the highest honor and authority (verse 13). Having triumphed on the cross and accomplished the work of redemption, he now intercedes before the Father in order to complete the saving effects of his sacrifice in the lives of every person. The angels, who are ministering servants of the Son, honor Christ by helping his people attain salvation (verse 14).

Reflection and discussion

- Why might the preacher be comparing the Son of God to the angels?

- What is the role of the angels in relationship to Jesus Christ?

- Which quotation gives me the most confidence in the saving power of the Son of God?

Prayer

Heavenly Father, you have sent your divine Son to redeem the world and to reign forever as the Lord of your kingdom. Although I will perish like worn-out clothing, I trust that I will inherit salvation through the cross and resurrection of Jesus Christ.

LESSON 3  SESSION 2

How can we escape if we neglect so great a salvation?
HEBREWS 2:3

The Urgency of the Son's Revelation

HEBREWS 2:1–4 ¹*Therefore we must pay greater attention to what we have heard, so that we do not drift away from it.* ²*For if the message declared through angels was valid, and every transgression or disobedience received a just penalty,* ³*how can we escape if we neglect so great a salvation? It was declared at first through the Lord, and it was attested to us by those who heard him,* ⁴*while God added his testimony by signs and wonders and various miracles, and by gifts of the Holy Spirit, distributed according to his will.*

When life becomes either increasingly difficult or more and more routine, Christians may fall either into fear or complacency; in both cases they may lose sight of the gift they have received. The preacher knew that the congregation needed a deeper reflection on what Christ has done for them so that they do not "drift away" from their formerly confident faith (verse 1). He wants to offer them confidence in the good news they have heard in order to rekindle and reinvigorate their belief.

"The message declared through angels" is Israel's Torah given to Moses at Mount Sinai (verse 2). Jewish tradition held that this revelation was transmitted by angels, as reflected in New Testament writings. Both Stephen (in Acts) and Paul assert that the law was established through the mediation of angels (Acts 7:53; Gal 3:19). This Torah was God's holy instructions describing how to remain in life-giving covenant with God and one another. For this reason, "every transgression or disobedience received a just penalty."

The preacher contrasts this message declared through angels with God's revelation announced directly through his Son (verse 3). "So great a salvation," the holy gospel, demands an even greater response. We have been offered a salvation that delivers us from the penalty of sin and allows us to share in the very life of God. If we neglect this great gift, we cannot escape the consequences. This good news of salvation was announced by Christ the Lord, through his preaching and ministry, and then "attested to us by those who heard him." The original hearers of this homily, like readers today, were not eyewitnesses to the earthly ministry of Jesus, but the gospel was confirmed by the testimony of witnesses going back to Jesus himself.

This saving message of so great a salvation is not only testified to by apostolic witnesses, but their words are verified by God "by signs and wonders and various miracles, and by gifts of the Holy Spirit" (verse 4). Jesus told his disciples not only to "proclaim the good news" but also to "cure the sick, raise the dead, cleanse the lepers, cast out demons" (Matt 10:7–8). The Acts of the Apostles testifies to many of these mighty deeds. They are "signs" because they point beyond themselves to Jesus and his victory over sin, sickness, and death. They are "wonders" because they evoke a response of awe and amazement as they demonstrate the power of God. The gifts of the Holy Spirit are also distributed by God to contribute in a variety of ways to the church's evangelizing mission. The letters of Paul testify to the diversity of these gifts—preaching, pastoring, prophesying, healing, teaching, and more.

A preacher cannot just tell his audience to believe and do good; rather, he must exhort and encourage his listeners at the level of their will. The community was tempted to drift away from God's revelation in his Son. Although they had received the message of the gospel, they were drifting from their experience of the power of the exalted Christ in their daily lives. The community must not only intellectually believe; they must also live the message they have heard. A believing community is manifested when people are healed, the oppressed are freed, forgiveness is experienced, and service is abundant. This is the kind of exhortation the preacher offers his hearers.

Reflection and discussion

- In what ways have I drifted away from the saving message I have heard?

- What experiences have brought me back to a greater confidence in the faith I received?

- How do I expect my study of Hebrews to reinvigorate my trust in God's revelation of his Son?

Prayer

Lord God, when I allow the struggles and pains of life to draw me away from a confident faith, minister to me through your saving word. May the power of your word draw me from neglect and doubt to a deeper experience of your Holy Spirit.

LESSON 4 **SESSION 2**

> He had to become like his brothers and sisters in every respect, so that he might be a merciful and faithful high priest in the service of God. HEBREWS 2:17

The Suffering and Exaltation of Jesus

HEBREWS 2:5–18 ⁵*Now God did not subject the coming world, about which we are speaking, to angels. ⁶But someone has testified somewhere,*

"What are human beings that you are mindful of them,
   or mortals, that you care for them?
⁷You have made them for a little while lower than the angels;
   you have crowned them with glory and honor,
   ⁸subjecting all things under their feet."

Now in subjecting all things to them, God left nothing outside their control. As it is, we do not yet see everything in subjection to them, ⁹but we do see Jesus, who for a little while was made lower than the angels, now crowned with glory and honor because of the suffering of death, so that by the grace of God he might taste death for everyone.

¹⁰It was fitting that God, for whom and through whom all things exist, in bringing many children to glory, should make the pioneer of their salvation perfect through sufferings. ¹¹For the one who sanctifies and those who are sanctified all have one Father. For this reason Jesus is not ashamed to call them brothers and sisters, ¹²saying,

"I will proclaim your name to my brothers and sisters,
   in the midst of the congregation I will praise you."

¹³And again,

"I will put my trust in him."

And again,

"Here am I and the children whom God has given me."

¹⁴Since, therefore, the children share flesh and blood, he himself likewise shared the same things, so that through death he might destroy the one who has the power of death, that is, the devil, ¹⁵and free those who all their lives were held in slavery by the fear of death. ¹⁶For it is clear that he did not come to help angels, but the descendants of Abraham. ¹⁷Therefore he had to become like his brothers and sisters in every respect, so that he might be a merciful and faithful high priest in the service of God, to make a sacrifice of atonement for the sins of the people. ¹⁸Because he himself was tested by what he suffered, he is able to help those who are being tested.

Formerly, according to Jewish tradition, God assigned angels to direct each nation of the world, with Michael as the archangel who guides Israel. But now, with God's decisive intervention in human history, God subjects "the coming world" to his exalted Son (verse 5). This new creation, which awaits its fullness, is now already present in Jesus. The whole world is being renewed and placed at the feet of the Son, who sits at the right hand of the Father.

The homilist invokes Psalm 8 to throw light on the mystery of Christ's incarnation and exultation. As the psalmist contemplates the majesty of the heavens, he expresses wonder at God's care for human beings (verse 6). Indeed, God has made them "for a little while lower than the angels" and has "crowned them with glory and honor," giving them royal authority over creation and subjecting everything to their control (verses 7–8).

Now, nothing could be more obvious than that God's lofty purposes for humanity are not yet fully realized. But the sovereignty that human beings have failed to exercise is already being wielded on their behalf by Jesus, who is the fullest realization of the ideals of the psalm (verse 9). In his incarnation, he stooped to a status "lower than the angels" to enter the human condition, and through his death, he is "now crowned with glory and honor." In the risen Jesus, clothed with divine majesty, we can already glimpse our own glorious future.

The fullest meaning of Psalm 8 has been brought to light by the gospel. By reading the hymn in and through Jesus Christ, the true representative of humanity, the homilist expresses the entire drama of redemption. The Son descended from the heights, down through the realm of the angels, into the depths of human suffering and death, then back upward into glory with all things subject to him. He is the new and final Adam, in whom God's original plan for human beings is restored and perfected. In him we see already what will one day be the exalted destiny of all humanity.

In describing God's plan to bring "many children to glory," the homilist describes Jesus Christ as the "pioneer" of salvation, blazing the trail along which God's many children would be brought to glory (verse 10). Yet for him to be humanity's representative and forerunner in the way of salvation, Jesus was made "perfect through sufferings." In order to be the perfect Savior for his brothers and sisters, he must experience the depths of the human condition—loneliness, rejection, pain, and death. By willingly undergoing his passion, Jesus allowed all the suffering unleashed upon him to refine his human nature to perfection and to bring forth the most perfect act of obedience, trust, and love that could ever come from a human heart.

The preacher continues to express the solidarity of God's Son with God's sons and daughters, "the one who sanctifies and those who are sanctified" (verse 11). Three quotes from the Old Testament reinforce this solidarity, interpreting each as spoken by Jesus (verses 12–13). United in the "flesh and blood" of humanity, the Son of God became one with us in the most radical way possible (verse 14). In his bodily crucifixion and death, Christ achieved two great victories: first, he conquered death by dying, destroying its power from within, and second, he freed humanity from the slavery brought about by our fear of death (verse 15). This paralyzing fear leads us to resist anything that reminds us of our mortality: weakness, failure, criticism, deprivation, separation, loss, sickness, aging, and more. Freedom from this fear enables the Christian, even now, to live in the expectant joy of resurrection.

The reason Christ had to become "like his brothers and sisters in every respect" was in order that he might be "a merciful and faithful high priest" (verse 17). The author of Hebrews is the only New Testament writer who explicitly gives Jesus the title "high priest," and this understanding is the heart of his teaching about how we are saved. Because Jesus entered our human condition, was tested and perfected through suffering, and was obedient to his divine mission to the end, he offered a perfect sacrifice of atonement for the sins of humanity.

Reflection and discussion
- In what ways does my suffering perfect me?

- Knowing that Jesus himself experienced the depths of human pain and struggle, what confidence or hope does this offer me?

- What does it mean to me that Christ has conquered the power of death?

Prayer
Pioneer of my salvation, help me to follow the way of salvation you have blazed before me. Let me know that the struggles of the human condition are the path to perfection and glory with you.

LESSON 5 **SESSION 2**

> Jesus is worthy of more glory than Moses, just as the builder of a house has more honor than the house itself. HEBREWS 3:3

The Faithful Son Placed over the House of God

HEBREWS 3:1–6 ¹*Therefore, brothers and sisters, holy partners in a heavenly calling, consider that Jesus, the apostle and high priest of our confession,* ²*was faithful to the one who appointed him, just as Moses also "was faithful in all God's house."* ³*Yet Jesus is worthy of more glory than Moses, just as the builder of a house has more honor than the house itself.* ⁴*(For every house is built by someone, but the builder of all things is God.)* ⁵*Now Moses was faithful in all God's house as a servant, to testify to the things that would be spoken later.* ⁶*Christ, however, was faithful over God's house as a son, and we are his house if we hold firm the confidence and the pride that belong to hope.*

The preacher continues to exhort listeners by emphasizing his solidarity with them. As God's children they are "brothers and sisters," and as sanctified by Christ they are "holy partners" in life's pilgrimage (verse 1). He urges them to contemplate the true significance of Jesus as both "apostle and high priest." Although the New Testament names many apostles (those who are "sent"), Jesus is the supreme apostle, sent by God. The truth we confess as Christians has been delivered by Jesus as apostle and accomplished by Jesus as high priest. As the one sent by God, Jesus represents God to humanity; as high priest, he represents humanity to God. In both senses, Jesus is the ideal mediator between God and humanity.

The text holds up two figures for us—Moses and Jesus—both of whom are "faithful" to God (verse 2). Then the author describes how Jesus is worthy of more glory than Moses (verse 3), in a comparison similar to that of Jesus and the angels in the first chapter. It may seem strange that the author would diminish Moses in order to magnify Jesus, given the strong Jewish character of the audience. In the eyes of Jesus and the apostles, Moses was the Old Testament figure who was held in greatest esteem. It is common, however, in the New Testament to describe the primacy of Jesus over key figures of the Hebrew Scriptures: Abraham (John 8:53, 58), Jacob (John 4:12), Moses (2 Cor 3:7–18), David (Matt 22:45), and Solomon (Matt 12:42). The purpose is not to diminish the importance of these key figures but to indicate that the person and mission of Jesus shines brighter, just as the stars diminish when the sun rises.

The principal point of the passage, however, centers on us—the church. In the Old Testament the "house" of God is often a metaphor for the people of God (Num 12:7), a vast household embracing many generations. The author does not describe two houses, one old and one new. Rather, the house of God is the people of Israel united with the Christian community. In this house, Moses functioned as a faithful servant (verse 5), but Jesus now functions as the Son of the house's founder (verse 6). Moses was the servant of something greater than himself—of God's plan that would be revealed in the future. Whereas Jesus is the fulfillment of the divine plan, the one who governs, protects, and inherits this house of God.

At the climax of this passage, the author proclaims, "We are his house" (verse 6). We are the people of God, the community of faith, the recipients of the salvation brought by Christ. But membership in God's house must not be taken for granted. The danger of drifting away through neglect is ever present. We must "hold firm the confidence and the pride that belong to hope." Faithfulness is required not only of Moses and Jesus but of all God's people as well.

Reflection and discussion

- What does the preacher say about Jesus by calling him both "apostle and high priest"?

- What are the implications for me in thinking about the church as the house of God? Does it give me greater confidence, pride, and hope?

- How does this exhortation encourage me to remain faithful to the Christian call and not drift away through neglect?

Prayer

Jesus, I know that you are the Son of God and brother to me. Help me to accept all my brothers and sisters in the church as your family, living with me in your house. Keep us faithful and confident in the calling we have received.

LESSON 6 SESSION 2

Exhort one another every day, as long as it is called "today," so that none of you may be hardened by the deceitfulness of sin. HEBREWS 3:13

Be Faithful as Partners of Christ

HEBREWS 3:7–19

⁷Therefore, as the Holy Spirit says,
"Today, if you hear his voice,
⁸do not harden your hearts as in the rebellion,
   as on the day of testing in the wilderness,
⁹where your ancestors put me to the test,
   though they had seen my works ¹⁰for forty years.
Therefore I was angry with that generation,
   and I said, 'They always go astray in their hearts,
   and they have not known my ways.'
¹¹As in my anger I swore,
   'They will not enter my rest.'"
¹²Take care, brothers and sisters, that none of you may have an evil, unbelieving heart that turns away from the living God. ¹³But exhort one another every day, as long as it is called "today," so that none of you may be hardened by the deceitfulness of sin. ¹⁴For we have become partners of Christ, if only we hold our first confidence firm to the end. ¹⁵As it is said,
"Today, if you hear his voice,
do not harden your hearts as in the rebellion."

¹⁶Now who were they who heard and yet were rebellious? Was it not all those who left Egypt under the leadership of Moses? ¹⁷But with whom was he angry forty years? Was it not those who sinned, whose bodies fell in the wilderness? ¹⁸And to whom did he swear that they would not enter his rest, if not to those who were disobedient? ¹⁹So we see that they were unable to enter because of unbelief.

It is difficult, day after day, to live as holy partners in our heavenly calling, to live as the "house of God" in the midst of the world, to remain faithful and hold firm in confidence and hope. We become disenchanted when we compare the flawed and sinful church to the perfect church of our imagination. As we can sometimes be, the community addressed by the preacher was discouraged and despondent, tempted to drift away through neglect. This homily is the preacher's attempt to rouse them to renewed fidelity.

The opening verses of this chapter compared Moses and Jesus, and more important, the people of God under Moses and the renewed people of God in Christ. These verses now offer the pattern of God's people under Moses in the wilderness as a warning to the church today. This was the generation that witnessed their deliverance from Egypt, crossed the sea on dry land, was fed by wondrous manna, and witnessed God's covenant at Sinai. Citing Psalm 95:7–11, the writer highlights the people's rebellion and their willingness to abandon God's invitation (verses 7–11). Like God's people who journeyed for forty years, the community addressed by the preacher is often tempted to give up, to grow despondent, to harden their hearts. They must avoid the mistakes of their ancestors in the wilderness.

Instead, the people of God in Christ must focus on the "today" of faith (verses 13, 15). "Today" is the present time, the critical moment for faith; it is every day lived one day at a time.

God's people are called not only to hear God's words from the past but also to be attentive to his living voice addressing us in the present. We tend to take lightly the daily gifts we receive and dismiss the daily word of God given to us. When we look too far to the past or the future, we lose sight of this moment. The preacher urges us to exhort, encourage, and counsel one another every day, day after day, so that when some falter in faith, they are upheld by others.

Under Moses, the people rebelled and tested God, and thus were barred from entering the promised land (verses 16–19). If they failed, what is to keep us from failing? The consequences of disobedience and unbelief are just as momentous for us as for our ancestors. The key for Christians, however, is the fact that we are "partners of Christ" (verse 14). Despite our own weakness and sin, we share in Jesus' own faithfulness, if only we hold firmly to the confidence we experienced when we came to know him as our Lord. Let us learn to trust not in ourselves but in Jesus so as not to forfeit the blessed inheritance we have been given.

Reflection and discussion

- Psalm 95 is introduced with the words "the Holy Spirit says" (verse 7). How can I read this psalm and all Scripture not just as a word from the past but as the voice of the Holy Spirit speaking today?

- How is my life like that of God's people under Moses in the wilderness? What is the main difference?

- In what ways do I exhort and encourage others each day, as the preacher urges (verse 13)? What opportunities do I have to be encouraged to live faithfully in Christ?

Prayer

Faithful God, help me to hear your voice today and to trust that you are with me in life's wilderness. Give me the strength to remain faithful, the desire to encourage others, and the will to hold steadfast to the end.

SUGGESTIONS FOR FACILITATORS, GROUP SESSION 2

1. If there are newcomers who were not present for the first group session, introduce them now.

2. You may want to pray this prayer as a group:
   Faithful God, after speaking in many ways throughout the history of salvation, you have sent your divine Son to redeem the world and to reign forever as the Lord of your kingdom. When we allow the struggles and pains of life to draw us away from a confident faith, draw us through your saving word from neglect and doubt to a deeper experience of your Holy Spirit. Let us hear your voice today and trust that you are with us in life's wilderness. Give us the strength to remain faithful, to encourage others, and to hold steadfast to the end.

3. Ask one or more of the following questions:
   - What was your biggest challenge in Bible study over this past week?
   - What did you learn about yourself this week?

4. Discuss lessons 1 through 6 together. Assuming that group members have read the Scripture and commentary during the week, there is no need to read it aloud. As you review each lesson, you might want to briefly summarize the Scripture passages of each lesson and ask the group what stands out most clearly from the commentary.

5. Choose one or more of the questions for reflection and discussion from each lesson to talk over as a group. You may want to ask group members which question was most challenging or helpful to them as you review each lesson.

6. Keep the discussion moving, but don't rush the discussion in order to complete more questions. Allow time for the questions that provoke the most discussion.

7. Instruct group members to complete lessons 7 through 12 on their own during the six days before the next group meeting. They should write out their own answers to the questions as preparation for next week's group discussion.

8. Conclude by praying aloud together the prayer at the end of lesson 6, or any other prayer you choose.

LESSON 7 **SESSION 3**

> A sabbath rest still remains for the people of God;
> for those who enter God's rest also cease from their labors
> as God did from his. HEBREWS 4:9–10

The Rest that God Promised

HEBREWS 4:1–11 ¹*Therefore, while the promise of entering his rest is still open, let us take care that none of you should seem to have failed to reach it. ²For indeed the good news came to us just as to them; but the message they heard did not benefit them, because they were not united by faith with those who listened. ³For we who have believed enter that rest, just as God has said,*

> *"As in my anger I swore,*
> *'They shall not enter my rest,'"*

though his works were finished at the foundation of the world. ⁴For in one place it speaks about the seventh day as follows, "And God rested on the seventh day from all his works." ⁵And again in this place it says, "They shall not enter my rest." ⁶Since therefore it remains open for some to enter it, and those who formerly received the good news failed to enter because of disobedience, ⁷again he sets a certain day—"today"—saying through David much later, in the words already quoted,

> *"Today, if you hear his voice,*
> *do not harden your hearts."*

⁸For if Joshua had given them rest, God would not speak later about another day. ⁹So then, a sabbath rest still remains for the people of God; ¹⁰for those who enter God's rest also cease from their labors as God did from his. ¹¹Let us therefore make every effort to enter that rest, so that no one may fall through such disobedience as theirs.

The preacher continues to exhort his audience through the words of Psalm 95, showing them how they are not only to hear God's word from the past but to be attentive to God's living word in the present. Here he focuses on God's "rest," a word that occurs several times in these few verses. The rest of God, the rest to which God's people are called, represents the will of God brought to completion. Thus, we are reminded of the creation account of Genesis, "And God rested on the seventh day from all his works," which points to God's own sabbath rest on the final day of creation (verse 4). So, at the end of every week, the people of Israel remembered this "rest" of God by celebrating the sabbath as a day of quiet confidence in God, recalling God's past work and anticipating the future completion of God's plan of redemption, when the will of God will be fully realized in the age to come.

The preacher's exhortation focuses on God's rest as it is expressed in Psalm 95: "They shall not enter my rest" (verses 3, 5). For God's people in the wilderness, the "rest" was the promised land. The first generation under Moses did not enter into God's rest because of their infidelity and disobedience (verse 6). But for the listeners of the homily, the rest of God is still ahead of us as a goal to achieve, a promise in which to hope (verse 1). The failure of the wilderness generation serves as a warning for the present generation to keep reaching for the promise of entering God's rest.

The will of God is not yet complete: "A sabbath rest still remains for the people of God" (verse 9). All that came before in salvation history—God's rest on the seventh day of creation, the sabbath rest, the rest in the promised land—foreshadows the complete fulfillment of God's will for humanity, our sharing in divine life. Our ancestors heard "the good news" just as we have: for them the message of their deliverance at the exodus, and for us the message of the saving cross of Jesus. For both communities the good news is God's merciful love demonstrated in his redeeming actions (verse 2). But the message heard by the generation in the wilderness was of no value to them because they did not receive it with faith. For us the message is clear: our hearing the gospel must be accompanied by a steadfast and trusting faith in God's promises.

Again, the focus for the preacher is the present moment: "Today, if you hear his voice, do not harden your hearts" (verse 7). If God's rest had been achieved in the promised land under Joshua, then God would not have extended its offer through David in Psalm 95 or through the preacher in

Hebrews. "Today" is every day, listening to the living word of God. We enter God's rest today as we receive the good news, accept it with confident faith, and experience our present salvation in Christ. We rest from our labors, as God did from his, in the sense that we enter into the peace, security, and intimate communion that we will enjoy with God forever (verse 10).

The section concludes as it began, with an urgent exhortation: "while the promise of entering his rest is still open" (verse 1), "let us therefore make every effort to enter that rest" (verse 11). The author maintains the tension between the indicative (we are entering into God's rest) and the imperative (strive to enter that rest). The author's pastoral urgency counteracts the spiritual complacency of his audience that could cause them to drift away. Admonishing them not to fail like their ancestors, he presses them to be vigilant, not only for their own salvation but for that of their fellow Christians.

Reflection and discussion
- How does the commandment to honor the sabbath remind God's people of life's meaning and their priorities?

- What is the "rest" that the preacher urges us to make every effort to enter?

Prayer
Lord God, you have brought us the good news of your love demonstrated in your redeeming actions. Keep me from neglect and complacency as I strive to participate in your perfect rest.

LESSON 8   **SESSION 3**

> We do not have a high priest who is unable to sympathize with our weaknesses, but we have one who in every respect has been tested.
> HEBREWS 4:15

Jesus Is the Great High Priest

HEBREWS 4:12–16 ¹²*Indeed, the word of God is living and active, sharper than any two-edged sword, piercing until it divides soul from spirit, joints from marrow; it is able to judge the thoughts and intentions of the heart.* ¹³*And before him no creature is hidden, but all are naked and laid bare to the eyes of the one to whom we must render an account.*

¹⁴*Since, then, we have a great high priest who has passed through the heavens, Jesus, the Son of God, let us hold fast to our confession.* ¹⁵*For we do not have a high priest who is unable to sympathize with our weaknesses, but we have one who in every respect has been tested as we are, yet without sin.* ¹⁶*Let us therefore approach the throne of grace with boldness, so that we may receive mercy and find grace to help in time of need.*

As the preacher has shown through his discussion of Psalm 95 and many other passages from the ancient Scriptures, "the word of God is living and active" (verse 12). He urges his listeners to listen to God's voice today, for it is not a revelation confined to the past but a divine revelation that encounters us in the present. This word of God, like the sharpest of swords, can pierce to the very core of the human person, penetrating into its deepest and most hidden aspects. It can even reveal all the motives and desires that we hide, resist, and ignore in our hearts.

The sword of God's word is "two-edged" because it can either save us or convict us. It can penetrate any armor by which we try to hide from God's love, show us our desperate need for God's mercy, and cut away whatever inhibits God's grace within us. Because of the probing power of God's word, nothing within us can be concealed from God (verse 13). All of us must "render an account" to God for the choices we make and the lives we lead. Because of this urgency, there is no room for neglect and complacency with regard to our lives in Christ.

The unsettling image of God's word as a piercing sword enables us to recognize our need for Jesus, the "great high priest" (verse 14). The homilist urges the congregation to "hold fast" to their confession of faith in the face of any wavering or drifting away. This high priesthood of Jesus is unique in that he is both divine and human, the one "who has passed through the heavens" and who is able to "sympathize with our weaknesses" (verse 15). In his divine nature, he is the Son of God; in his humanity, Jesus experienced the full range of temptations just like us, yet unlike us he never yielded to sin. As truly God and fully human, he alone is capable of overcoming the great chasm between the holy God and sinful humanity.

The Old Testament had already revealed a God who enters personally into relationship with human beings, who loves them intensely and grieves over their injustice, ingratitude, and unfaithfulness. This is a God who is tender and merciful toward his people, and who is even jealous when his people stray from the covenant and seek other gods. But the fact that God would enter personally into our human experiences, even suffering and dying for us, was totally unlike any previous understanding of God. In the incarnation, the word of God has become flesh, the Son of God has placed himself in total solidarity with us. The fact that Jesus is now exalted to the heavens and dwells with the Father does not cancel his humanity. He is and remains always fully human, and he understands all our weaknesses, temptations, infirmities, and limitations from within.

This confession of faith enables us to "approach the throne of grace with boldness" (verse 16). In the former covenant God's people were able to draw near to him through priesthood, temple, and sacrifice. But there was still an unbridgeable divide between God and his people, symbolized by the veil that denied access to the holy of holies to everyone except the high priest once each year. Now, through the death and resurrection of Jesus, the way is opened for all people to enter God's holy presence. We can confidently approach God's throne to receive divine mercy and God's grace for our every need.

Reflection and discussion
- How have I experienced God's word as sharper and more piercing than a sword?

- In what ways do I allow God's word to penetrate and transform my heart?

- How does the humanity of the glorified Jesus give me confidence when I approach the throne of God?

Prayer
Merciful High Priest, let the word of God penetrate my body, soul, mind, and heart so that I may be transformed from within. Bring my daily prayers, works, joys, and sufferings to the throne of grace to be joined with your perfect offering.

LESSON 9 SESSION 3

Christ did not glorify himself in becoming a high priest, but was appointed by the one who said to him, "You are my Son, today I have begotten you."
HEBREWS 5:5

The High Priest in the Old and New Covenants

HEBREWS 5:1–10 *¹Every high priest chosen from among mortals is put in charge of things pertaining to God on their behalf, to offer gifts and sacrifices for sins. ²He is able to deal gently with the ignorant and wayward, since he himself is subject to weakness; ³and because of this he must offer sacrifice for his own sins as well as for those of the people. ⁴And one does not presume to take this honor, but takes it only when called by God, just as Aaron was.*

⁵So also Christ did not glorify himself in becoming a high priest, but was appointed by the one who said to him,

"You are my Son,
today I have begotten you";
⁶as he says also in another place,
"You are a priest forever,
according to the order of Melchizedek."

⁷In the days of his flesh, Jesus offered up prayers and supplications, with loud cries and tears, to the one who was able to save him from death, and he was heard because of his reverent submission. ⁸Although he was a Son, he learned obedience through what he suffered; ⁹*and having been made perfect, he became the source of eternal salvation for all who obey him,* ¹⁰*having been designated by God a high priest according to the order of Melchizedek.*

The homilist begins a discussion of the high priesthood by describing its essential characteristics in the old covenant. A high priest is defined as one who is "chosen from among mortals," who on behalf of them "is put in charge of things pertaining to God," and who offers to God "gifts and sacrifices for sins" (verse 1). In other words, a high priest is a mediator, the people's representative before God, chosen to make offerings to God in atonement for sins. Furthermore, a high priest "is able to deal gently with the ignorant and wayward" since he himself is prone to the very same sins (verse 2). Because he is beset by weakness, he must offer sacrifices for his own sins first, and then for the sins of the people (verse 3). Finally, the office of high priest is an honor that one does not presume for oneself but receives it "only when called by God" (verse 4).

Aaron, the brother of Moses and first high priest, demonstrates all of these crucial features. God designated Aaron and his descendants within the tribe of Levi to serve as Israel's priests. But shortly after that divine appointment, Aaron played a lead role in Israel's initial sin, the disastrous idolatry of the golden calf. For this reason, both at the rite of priestly ordination and the annual Day of Atonement, the priest must offer sacrifice first for his own sins before making offerings for the community (Lev 9:8, 15; 16:6).

In Jesus Christ a transformation of Israel's priesthood takes place. But only in light of this background on priesthood in the Torah is it possible to appreciate this change. Jesus is both similar and dissimilar to the previous high priests. On the one hand, Jesus exemplifies all that priesthood represented in the old covenant, but on the other hand, Jesus embodies it in an astonishingly new way. Hebrews demonstrates how Jesus both fulfills and surpasses each aspect of Israel's priesthood.

Like the former high priests, Jesus did not undertake his mission at his own initiative; he was "appointed" by the Father (verse 5). The uniqueness of this divine commissioning and the singularly new priesthood of Jesus are demonstrated through juxtaposing texts from two royal psalms that the early Christians understood as prophecies of the promised Messiah and Son of David. The first, "You are my Son, today I have begotten you" (see Ps 2:7), points to Christ's divine sonship and his messianic kingship. As the divine Son, he has the closest possible union with God, a unity necessary for priesthood. The second, "You are a priest forever, according to the order of Melchizedek" (Ps 110:4), points to Christ's divine appointment as an eternal priest, in the line of Melchizedek, who was both a king and a priest.

Jesus is certainly not just one more priest like Aaron, offering animal sacrifices in the temple. Jesus, like all the royal sons of David, belongs to the tribe of Judah, not the priestly tribe of Levi. So how can Jesus be a priest? The psalm highlights another valid priesthood in saving history, revealed far earlier than the priesthood of Aaron established at Mount Sinai. This ancient priesthood, which the tradition calls "the order of Melchizedek," derives from the mysterious priest-king of Salem who blessed Abraham and offered bread and wine (Gen 14:18–20). The psalm proposes that this royal priesthood belongs to the kings in the line of David and is embodied most perfectly in the Messiah. Furthermore, the reality that Melchizedek was a Gentile suggests that his priesthood is universal and not limited to the people of Israel. This priesthood of the order of Melchizedek is the eternal and universal priesthood of Jesus Christ (verse 10).

When a man was made a priest under the former covenant, he had to be separated from ordinary people in order to relate to God. But when the Son of God was made high priest, it was his solidarity with the rest of humanity that needed to be assured. He had to become like his brothers and sisters in every respect. Although Christ had no sin and thus had no need to offer sacrifice for himself, he embodied the full range of human experiences. In the final hours of his earthly life, "Jesus offered up prayers and supplications, with loud cries and tears" to the Father (verse 7). At his agony in Gethsemane, throughout his passion, to his death on the cross, Jesus pleaded not to be spared from death but rather to be free of death's power over him. His pain, sorrows, and pleading became an essential part of his priestly sacrifice as he handed over his life completely in love. Indeed, obedience, wisdom, and love, like all virtues, come to perfection while being tested in the crucible of suffering (verses 8–9).

Through the Son's "reverent submission" God heard his prayers, and his sacrifice on the cross was made worthy of divine glory. On the cross, Jesus shone as the eternal and universal high priest, becoming "the source of eternal salvation for all who obey him." As we offer our needs, our pains, our joys, our cries, our longings, and our thanksgiving to God, Jesus the high priest unites them with his own perfect sacrifice to the Father.

Reflection and discussion

- In what ways is the high priesthood of Jesus similar to that of the high priests of ancient Israel?

- How does the author show that the priesthood of Jesus is eternal and universal?

- How does an understanding of the priesthood of Jesus deepen my appreciation of his suffering and death?

Prayer

High Priest of the new covenant, you have become like us in every respect and entered into the full range of our human experiences. As our perfect mediator, teach me to offer my prayers, works, joys, and sufferings united with your perfect sacrifice to the Father.

LESSON 10  SESSION 3

> Though by this time you ought to be teachers, you need someone
> to teach you again the basic elements of the oracles of God.
> HEBREWS 5:12

Moving from Infancy to Maturity in Faith

HEBREWS 5:11—6:3 ¹¹*About this we have much to say that is hard to explain, since you have become dull in understanding.* ¹²*For though by this time you ought to be teachers, you need someone to teach you again the basic elements of the oracles of God. You need milk, not solid food;* ¹³*for everyone who lives on milk, being still an infant, is unskilled in the word of righteousness.* ¹⁴*But solid food is for the mature, for those whose faculties have been trained by practice to distinguish good from evil.*

6 ¹*Therefore let us go on toward perfection, leaving behind the basic teaching about Christ, and not laying again the foundation: repentance from dead works and faith toward God,* ²*instruction about baptisms, laying on of hands, resurrection of the dead, and eternal judgment.* ³*And we will do this, if God permits.*

After introducing the topic of Christ's priesthood in new covenant worship, the preacher lets his audience know that he still has much to teach them about this topic, truths that are "hard to explain" (verse 11). He will indeed continue this important and difficult teaching later, but for now, he pauses to interject a long exhortation. He accuses his audience of becoming "dull in understanding" and closing themselves to the more challenging truths he wants them to grasp. This sounds similar to the exasperation of Jesus with his disciples as he quotes from the prophet Isaiah: "This people's heart has grown dull, and their ears are hard of hearing, and they have shut their eyes" (Matt 13:15).

Although they ought to be able to teach the Christian faith to others by this time, they seem unready to learn more (verse 12). They don't even remember "the basic elements of the oracles of God" and need to be taught again the rudiments of the Christian faith. The author compares food for babies (milk) and food for adults (solid food), a metaphor used also by Paul (1 Cor 3:2). Drinking milk or being nursed is appropriate for people who are newly reborn in Christ. But after years have passed, Christians ought to be able to digest solid food, teachings that will deepen their understanding of the faith (verses 13–14).

Through the regular practice of studying God's word and being formed by it, Christians grow in Christian maturity. By training their mind and will, they become more skilled in understanding and practice. They are able to receive more advanced teachings, discern moral choices, and instruct beginners by word and example. Those who refuse to grow up and continue learning remain stuck in an immature faith and fail to take on adult responsibilities in the Christian life.

There are two ways to move in the Christian life: toward a deeper understanding and experience of the truths of faith or into a lethargic laxity. The preacher exhorts his listeners to move on, to strive toward greater perfection in Christ (verse 1). He urges them to build on the foundational teachings of the Christian life, although sometimes those who have grown lax in their spiritual growth need to be retaught these fundamentals before going on to more difficult matters in the Christian life. The "basic teaching about Christ" consists of three pairs: repentance from a worldly life and confident faith in God; baptismal instructions and "laying on of hands" (thus invoking the gifts of the Holy Spirit); and belief in resurrection and the final judgment of our lives to determine our eternal destiny (verse 2). These elements summarize the foundations featured in the church's earliest preaching as recorded in the Acts of the Apostles.

By suggesting that his hearers are sluggish, the preacher tries to sharpen their attention and whet their appetites for what he will teach them next. In this way he stimulates their resolve to move beyond the basics to more solid spiritual food. "We will do this," he urges confidently, "if God permits" (verse 3). Although maturing in the faith requires dedication and resolve, our lives are totally dependent on God's providence. The Holy Spirit instills both the divine grace and the desire within our hearts to mature in Christ.

Reflection and discussion
- At what level am I in my understanding of the truths of faith? What are some ways I can attain a deeper understanding and mature in my faith?

- Do I feel capable of teaching the basics of the Christian faith to others?

- How can I encourage my own family and community toward a deeper maturity in Christ?

Prayer
Master teacher, you have given me the gift of faith, but it is my responsibility to seek deeper understanding and growth. When I become weak in understanding and lax in my resolve, challenge me toward greater progress in your word.

LESSON 11 SESSION 3

God is not unjust; he will not overlook your work and the love that you showed for his sake in serving the saints, as you still do. HEBREWS 6:10

Remain Faithful until Hope Is Fulfilled

HEBREWS 6:4–12 ⁴*For it is impossible to restore again to repentance those who have once been enlightened, and have tasted the heavenly gift, and have shared in the Holy Spirit, ⁵and have tasted the goodness of the word of God and the powers of the age to come, ⁶and then have fallen away, since on their own they are crucifying again the Son of God and are holding him up to contempt. ⁷Ground that drinks up the rain falling on it repeatedly, and that produces a crop useful to those for whom it is cultivated, receives a blessing from God. ⁸But if it produces thorns and thistles, it is worthless and on the verge of being cursed; its end is to be burned over.*
⁹*Even though we speak in this way, beloved, we are confident of better things in your case, things that belong to salvation. ¹⁰For God is not unjust; he will not overlook your work and the love that you showed for his sake in serving the saints, as you still do. ¹¹And we want each one of you to show the same diligence so as to realize the full assurance of hope to the very end, ¹²so that you may not become sluggish, but imitators of those who through faith and patience inherit the promises.*

Having urged his listeners to move beyond the fundamentals of the Christian life and "go on toward perfection" (6:1), the preacher issues a severe warning to those who may fall away and reject the gift of salvation. The danger of apostasy, abandoning belief in Christ, is particularly acute for those who remain in a lax and immature faith, neglecting to move toward maturity. For the preacher says it is "impossible" for those who have truly experienced Christ and the new life he offers to fall away and then be brought to repentance again (verse 4).

The Christian life is described with five phrases, each of which is highly experiential in its emphasis. For life in Christ is far more than just taking on a new set of beliefs; it is an intense experience of new and transformed life. Christians are, first, those who have "been enlightened"; that is, their minds, which were formerly trapped in the darkness of ignorance and sin, have been illumined by Christ. Second, Christians have "tasted the heavenly gift"; that is, they have experienced the abundant graces and blessings that God bestows. Third, they have "shared in the Holy Spirit"; that is, God's own Spirit has come to dwell within them and bestow spiritual gifts upon them. Fourth, Christians have "tasted the goodness of the word of God," experiencing its transforming effects, whether proclaimed in liturgy, taught to them, or read in prayerful devotion (verse 5). Finally, they have tasted "the powers of the age to come," the wonders that God is working in the world, signs that the age to come has arrived in Christ.

People raised in the Christian faith reject it for a variety of different reasons. Often they have never really heard the good news in a way that made sense to them, or they have never truly experienced the reality of faith and salvation in a way that was real and personal for them. It is one thing when people turn away who have never fully known or understood the faith, when they have only skimmed the surface. It is sad when such people leave the church but not necessarily tragic. There is always a chance that they will return at some later point when they have experienced more of life and are ready to truly embrace the person and message of Christ.

It is a totally different matter when someone who has experienced the depths of faith rejects that gift. When a person has truly tasted salvation, shared in the gifts of the Holy Spirit, comprehended God's word, heard God speaking inside, experienced grace personally—life is never the same again. Practically speaking such a person cannot reject that gift and then hope to repent and experience it again. Apostates have rejected the very basis of salvation and aligned themselves with the enemies of Christ. Figuratively they are crucifying the Lord again, and as others witness their disloyalty, they are holding him up to disgrace and ridicule (verse 6). Abandoning the Christian faith is comparable to soil that produces "thorns and thistles," a worthless and destructive yield, whereas authentic faith is equivalent to good soil that absorbs the rain and produces a blessed and beneficial yield (verses 7–8).

Although rebuke and warning is necessary, the preacher's main intent is to praise and encourage the community. He expresses confidence in their perseverance and fidelity, assuring them that God will remember the loving service they have shown in the past and will sustain them through their present struggles (verses 9–10). With the heart of a pastor, he urges them to remain diligent and not become sluggish, traveling their pilgrimage of faith toward its goal, holding on to their hope in God (verses 11–12).

Reflection and discussion
- Is it absolutely "impossible" or practically "impossible" for a Christian to fall away from faith and then to repent and return to Christ? See Mark 10:27.

- How profoundly have I "tasted the heavenly gift" of salvation? Am I skimming the surface of faith, or am I accepting the depths of what Christ offers me?

- Why does the preacher feel the need to offer both stern admonition and gentle encouragement?

Prayer
Father, as the rain of your word penetrates the rich soil of my life, help me absorb your grace and bring forth a crop of abundant love and service. May I increasingly taste your heavenly gift of salvation.

LESSON 12  SESSION 3

Seize the hope set before us. We have this hope, a sure and steadfast anchor of the soul. HEBREWS 6:18–19

Hope in God's Steadfast Promises

HEBREWS 6:13–20 ¹³When God made a promise to Abraham, because he had no one greater by whom to swear, he swore by himself, ¹⁴saying, "I will surely bless you and multiply you." ¹⁵And thus Abraham, having patiently endured, obtained the promise. ¹⁶Human beings, of course, swear by someone greater than themselves, and an oath given as confirmation puts an end to all dispute. ¹⁷In the same way, when God desired to show even more clearly to the heirs of the promise the unchangeable character of his purpose, he guaranteed it by an oath, ¹⁸so that through two unchangeable things, in which it is impossible that God would prove false, we who have taken refuge might be strongly encouraged to seize the hope set before us. ¹⁹We have this hope, a sure and steadfast anchor of the soul, a hope that enters the inner shrine behind the curtain, ²⁰where Jesus, a forerunner on our behalf, has entered, having become a high priest forever according to the order of Melchizedek.

To the community addressed by the preacher, life in Christ must have felt like a boat on a turbulent sea, as it has seemed for Christians throughout history. For his audience and for us, the author wants to assure his hearers that God's promises are absolutely reliable and that our hope is anchored in this trustworthiness of God. The promises God made to our ancestor Abraham also belong to us, as Abraham's children. God has not changed course, and his purposes have not been altered.

For Jewish Christians of this community, Abraham is an ideal model of one who inherited the promises after waiting in hope. God's promise of many descendants to Abraham was tested when God asked him to sacrifice his son, who seemed to be the only fulfillment of that promise. God not only spared Isaac and renewed the promise, but God did so with an oath (Gen 22:16–18). The author's summary of God's promise, "I will surely bless you and multiply you," represents the entire content of God's covenant. Abraham's patient endurance, through his many trials, led to his obtaining the promise (verse 15). However, his receiving the promise must refer only to the first signs of fulfillment, since Abraham and the other heroes of the old covenant did not obtain the fullness of what God promised.

In the ancient Near East swearing an oath in the name of a god was a way of guaranteeing or giving solemn value to a promise. Though God's word was enough, God did something highly unusual in order to assure Abraham's descendants of the absolute steadfastness of the divine promises. God swore an oath in his own name, affirming "the unchangeable character of his purpose" (verses 16–17). Thus, "through two unchangeable things," God's promise and the renewal of God's promise with an oath, God is doubly bound to be faithful to the promises he first gave to Abraham. With this exceptional double affirmation, we can "seize the hope set before us" (verse 18). The author's Jewish-Christian hearers were given certain confidence that the new covenant in Jesus Christ involves not a departure from, but the fulfillment of, the divine promises upon which Israel has based its hopes.

Our hope rests not only in God's promises to our ancestors but in Jesus Christ, whose priestly sacrifice, his saving death and resurrection, ensures our salvation. This confident expectation is represented through the image of an anchor, which stabilizes a boat on a turbulent sea (verse 19). This "sure and steadfast anchor of the soul" will not allow the community to drift away but to remain firm and steady through their stormy trials.

The preacher prepares us for his continuing explanation of the high priestly service of Jesus, stating that Christ our hope "enters the inner shrine behind the curtain." This inner shrine refers to the holy of holies of God's temple, the imperfect shadow of which is in Jerusalem and the perfect reality of which is in heaven. Because the sacrificial death of Jesus has torn the curtain in two, from top to bottom (Mark 15:38), Jesus, "a forerunner on our behalf" (verse 20), has entered the sanctuary and offers us unrestricted entrance into God's presence.

Reflection and discussion

- Why would God, whose word is truth and whose promises are absolutely trustworthy, reconfirm his promise to Abraham by swearing an oath?

- How would the example of Abraham's patient trust help the hearers of Hebrews?

- What is testing my hope right now? How firmly anchored is my hope in God?

Prayer

Eternal God, you know my needs, my fears, and my lack of trust. May my hope of salvation be the steadfast anchor of my soul. Help me hold fast to that hope and receive the promises you have given me.

SUGGESTIONS FOR FACILITATORS, GROUP SESSION 3

1. Welcome group members and ask if there are any announcements anyone would like to make.

2. You may want to pray this prayer as a group:
   High Priest of the new covenant, who has become like us in every respect and entered into the full range of our human experiences, give us confidence in the good news of your love demonstrated in your redeeming actions. As our perfect mediator, bring our daily prayers, works, joys, and sufferings to the throne of divine grace to be joined with your perfect sacrifice. When we become weak in understanding and lax in our resolve, let the sacred Scriptures penetrate our bodies, souls, minds, and hearts, so that we may be transformed from within.

3. Ask one or more of the following questions:
   - Which thought from the lessons this week stands out most memorably to you?
   - What is the most important lesson you learned through your study this week?

4. Discuss lessons 7 through 12. Choose one or more of the questions for reflection and discussion from each lesson to discuss as a group. You may want to ask group members which question was most challenging or helpful to them as you review each lesson.

5. Remember that there are no definitive answers for these discussion questions. The insights of group members will add to the understanding of all. None of these questions require an expert.

6. After talking about each lesson, instruct group members to complete lessons 13 through 18 on their own during the six days before the next group meeting. They should write out their own answers to the questions as preparation for next week's group discussion.

7. Ask the group if anyone is having any particular problems with the Bible study during the week. You may want to share advice and encouragement within the group.

8. Conclude by praying aloud together the prayer at the end of one of the lessons discussed. You may add to the prayer based on the sharing that has occurred in the group.

LESSON 13 **SESSION 4**

> This man, who does not belong to their ancestry, collected tithes from Abraham and blessed him who had received the promises.
> HEBREWS 7:6

Melchizedek, the Priest and King

HEBREWS 7:1–10 ¹This "King Melchizedek of Salem, priest of the Most High God, met Abraham as he was returning from defeating the kings and blessed him"; ²and to him Abraham apportioned "one-tenth of everything." His name, in the first place, means "king of righteousness"; next he is also king of Salem, that is, "king of peace." ³Without father, without mother, without genealogy, having neither beginning of days nor end of life, but resembling the Son of God, he remains a priest forever.

⁴See how great he is! Even Abraham the patriarch gave him a tenth of the spoils. ⁵And those descendants of Levi who receive the priestly office have a commandment in the law to collect tithes from the people, that is, from their kindred, though these also are descended from Abraham. ⁶But this man, who does not belong to their ancestry, collected tithes from Abraham and blessed him who had received the promises. ⁷It is beyond dispute that the inferior is blessed by the superior. ⁸In the one case, tithes are received by those who are mortal; in the other, by one of whom it is testified that he lives. ⁹One might even say that Levi himself, who receives tithes, paid tithes through Abraham, ¹⁰for he was still in the loins of his ancestor when Melchizedek met him.

Following his extended exhortation, the preacher returns to his teaching about Jesus as the great high priest. In the next four chapters, the author will demonstrate how new covenant worship completes and perfects the priesthood, sacrifice, and all the institutions of worship under the old covenant. Jesus Christ himself establishes the new covenant, and in him the worship of God's people is perfected through his one, eternal, and universal sacrifice.

Having already introduced Melchizedek as a foreshadowing of the Messiah—"You are a priest forever, according to the order of Melchizedek" (Ps 110:4)—the author turns to the only other place in the Old Testament where Melchizedek appears: Genesis 14:18–20. Abraham has just defeated a coalition of four invading kings from the East, rescuing his nephew Lot and recovering other captives and plunder. Returning home, Abraham was met by "King Melchizedek of Salem, priest of the Most High God" (verse 1). This king-priest of the Canaanite city that later became Jerusalem brought out bread and wine to Abraham and blessed him. Amazingly, Melchizedek's blessing evokes the Most High God, the God of Abraham, who is both "maker of heaven and earth" and the one who "delivered your enemies into your hand!" (Gen 14:19–20). On his part, Abraham apportioned "one-tenth of everything," a tithe of all the spoils, to Melchizedek (verse 2).

The citation from Genesis shows how Melchizedek prefigures Christ as the royal and priestly Messiah. Like Melchizedek, the Son of God is a priest and a king, who offers bread and wine. As "king of righteousness" and "king of peace," Melchizedek epitomizes the most significant qualities of the promised Messiah. Furthermore, the fact that Scripture is silent about the lineage as well as the lifespan of Melchizedek offers the impression that his priesthood is continuous and unending. Thus, like the Son of God, "he remains a priest forever" (verse 3). In all these ways, our preacher looks back on the figure of Melchizedek as a prefiguration of Christ, a signpost that points toward the Messiah who will fulfill the ministry of the ancient king-priest of Salem. In this way, we realize that the good gifts we have been given in Jesus were in the mind of God from the beginnings of our salvation history.

The author continues to emphasize "how great" Melchizedek is, even in comparison to Abraham, the patriarch of all his descendants in Israel (verse 4). Because Abraham was blessed by Melchizedek and Abraham gave him "a tenth of the spoils," the priesthood of Melchizedek is certainly of an exceptional character. Centuries after Abraham, under Israel's Torah, those who received the priestly office were descendants of Levi. These inherited the priesthood from their fathers and passed it on to their sons. These levitical priests collected tithes and blessed their kindred, all descendants of Abraham (verse 5). The superiority of Melchizedek's priesthood is demonstrated by the fact that he blessed Abraham and received tithes from him (verse 6).

In fact, it may even be said that Levi, who received tithes from the Israelites, paid tithes through Abraham (verses 9–10). This argument is dependent on the biblical understanding that an ancestor contains within himself all his descendants. Since Levi is Abraham's great-grandson, it can be said that he paid tithes to Melchizedek too. In all these ways, the eternal priesthood of Melchizedek is prior and superior to the levitical priesthood of Israel, and thus, Jesus is not a priest of the line of Levi but an everlasting and universal priest "according to the order of Melchizedek."

Reflection and discussion
- What is significant about the fact that Melchizedek is both a priest and a king?

- What seems to be the main point of the author's comparison between Melchizedek and Abraham?

- How is the priesthood of Melchizedek shown to be superior to the priesthood of Levi and his descendants?

- What are some of the ways that Jesus Christ is prefigured by Melchizedek?

- Why is it necessary that the priesthood of Jesus be rooted in a different priesthood than the hereditary priesthood of the tribe of Levi?

Prayer
King of righteousness and peace, you established your reign upon the foundations of the kingdom of Israel. Help me to honor and revere Abraham and all my spiritual ancestors in the old covenant so that I may know you and serve your kingdom forever.

LESSON 14　　SESSION 4

> **He has no need to offer sacrifices day after day,
> first for his own sins, and then for those of the people;
> this he did once for all when he offered himself.**
> HEBREWS 7:27

A New High Priest Resembling Melchizedek

HEBREWS 7:11–28 ¹¹*Now if perfection had been attainable through the levitical priesthood—for the people received the law under this priesthood—what further need would there have been to speak of another priest arising according to the order of Melchizedek, rather than one according to the order of Aaron?* ¹²*For when there is a change in the priesthood, there is necessarily a change in the law as well.* ¹³*Now the one of whom these things are spoken belonged to another tribe, from which no one has ever served at the altar.* ¹⁴*For it is evident that our Lord was descended from Judah, and in connection with that tribe Moses said nothing about priests.*

¹⁵*It is even more obvious when another priest arises, resembling Melchizedek,* ¹⁶*one who has become a priest, not through a legal requirement concerning physical descent, but through the power of an indestructible life.* ¹⁷*For it is attested of him,*

"*You are a priest forever,
　according to the order of Melchizedek."*

¹⁸*There is, on the one hand, the abrogation of an earlier commandment because it was weak and ineffectual* ¹⁹*(for the law made nothing perfect); there is, on the other hand, the introduction of a better hope, through which we approach God.*

²⁰*This was confirmed with an oath; for others who became priests took their office without an oath,* ²¹*but this one became a priest with an oath, because of the one who said to him,*

> *"The Lord has sworn*
> *and will not change his mind,*
> *'You are a priest forever'"—*

²²*accordingly Jesus has also become the guarantee of a better covenant.*

²³*Furthermore, the former priests were many in number, because they were prevented by death from continuing in office;* ²⁴*but he holds his priesthood permanently, because he continues forever.* ²⁵*Consequently he is able for all time to save those who approach God through him, since he always lives to make intercession for them.*

²⁶*For it was fitting that we should have such a high priest, holy, blameless, undefiled, separated from sinners, and exalted above the heavens.* ²⁷*Unlike the other high priests, he has no need to offer sacrifices day after day, first for his own sins, and then for those of the people; this he did once for all when he offered himself.* ²⁸*For the law appoints as high priests those who are subject to weakness, but the word of the oath, which came later than the law, appoints a Son who has been made perfect forever.*

The "perfection" of which the preacher speaks is the completeness of God's will, the full realization of God's plan for the world (verse 11). Something greater and more lasting than the "levitical priesthood" was necessary. Furthermore, the law of Moses, under which the former priesthood developed, could not express the fullness of what God desires for his people (verse 12). Both the priesthood and the law had been established by God through Moses on Mount Sinai. All the detailed regulations about the levitical priesthood, the altar and sanctuary, and the many types of sacrifices pointed to a greater fulfillment.

The "perfection" of God's plan was reached in Jesus the Messiah, "the one of whom these things are spoken" (verse 13). But it was well-known in the early church that Jesus was from the royal line of David, from the tribe of Judah (verse 14). The law of Moses specified that Israel's priests must be descendants of Aaron, Israel's first high priest, from the tribe of Levi, and says nothing about priests from the tribe of Judah. For this reason, the preacher stresses that the priesthood of Jesus is not "according to the order of Aaron," but "according to the order of Melchizedek," the priest whose eternal and universal priesthood is prior and superior to that of Aaron.

The priesthood of Jesus Christ, foreshadowed by that of Melchizedek, does not develop from the legal requirements of the Torah but "arises" through the authority of his resurrection, "the power of an indestructible life" (verses 15–16). The one whom God appointed as king, "Sit at my right hand," is also the one whom God declared to be a priest, "You are a priest forever" (Ps 110:1, 4). Because Jesus now shares in God's life and power, he can raise us up to share in his own divine glory. The former regulations concerning the priesthood, temple, and sacrifice were "weak and ineffectual" in that they pointed toward a messianic completion (verse 18). But now, in the Messiah, the perfect priest-king of the new covenant, we have a "better hope" (verse 19). What the people of the old covenant had only in promise, we possess in its completed fullness. Whereas the people of Israel were forbidden to come near the sanctuary of God and were separated from God by the veil of the temple, we are able to approach God, enter the divine presence, and share deeply in divine life.

As the author declared that God's promise to Abraham was guaranteed by a divine oath (6:13–18), he states the same about God's declaration concerning the priesthood of the Messiah (verses 20–21). The perpetual priesthood of Jesus Christ is solemnly guaranteed: "The Lord has sworn and will not change his mind, 'You are a priest forever.'" Although the levitical priests took their office without an oath and held the office only until their death, the priesthood of Jesus is permanent because he lives and reigns forever (verses 23–24).

New covenant worship is centered in Jesus Christ as the perfect priest and mediator for all those who approach God through him (verse 25). Because he combines divinity and humanity perfectly in himself, he is the ideal intercessor for all who come to God. Through him, God draws near to us and we draw near to God in a way that is everlasting and unfailing. All other forms of new covenant priesthood—whether it be ordained ministerial priests or the universal priesthood of all Christian believers—are participations in the one priesthood of Christ.

Not only is Jesus the perfect priest, he is also the perfect sacrifice because "he offered himself" (verse 27). His whole life was a self-offering to the

Father, a sacrifice that reached its consummation on the cross. The sacrificial gift is the giver himself, a sin offering for all people; his saving power is available to all who desire to receive it. New covenant worship, then, is our participation in the sacrifice that Jesus Christ has offered for all people. Because both the priest and the sacrificial victim are perfect, the sacrifice is all-sufficient, eternally valid, and absolutely complete and effective. Although Jesus atoned for sin "once for all," we participate in his singular sacrifice as we offer our lives in union with his. In the Christian Eucharist, we participate in Christ's self-offering and receive its saving grace.

Reflection and discussion

- How does the fact that Jesus remains a priest forever make a difference in my trust before God?

- What are some of the ways in which Jesus is the perfect priest and the perfect sacrifice?

- How can I unite the offerings of my life to the one, perfect sacrifice of Jesus Christ?

Prayer

Divine High Priest, you intercede for us forever before God's throne. Help me to unite the daily sacrifices of my life—my prayers, works, joys, and sufferings—to your cross, so that my life may also become a sacrificial offering to the Father.

LESSON 15   SESSION 4

> Jesus has now obtained a more excellent ministry,
> and to that degree he is the mediator of a better covenant,
> which has been enacted through better promises.
> HEBREWS 8:6

High Priest of the New Covenant

HEBREWS 8:1–6 ¹*Now the main point in what we are saying is this: we have such a high priest, one who is seated at the right hand of the throne of the Majesty in the heavens,* ²*a minister in the sanctuary and the true tent that the Lord, and not any mortal, has set up.* ³*For every high priest is appointed to offer gifts and sacrifices; hence it is necessary for this priest also to have something to offer.* ⁴*Now if he were on earth, he would not be a priest at all, since there are priests who offer gifts according to the law.* ⁵*They offer worship in a sanctuary that is a sketch and shadow of the heavenly one; for Moses, when he was about to erect the tent, was warned, "See that you make everything according to the pattern that was shown you on the mountain."* ⁶*But Jesus has now obtained a more excellent ministry, and to that degree he is the mediator of a better covenant, which has been enacted through better promises.*

Entering into the heart of the homily, the preacher declares his main point: Jesus Christ is the true high priest, who possesses all the qualities of the eternal priesthood "according to the order of Melchizedek." He is seated in heavenly glory at God's "right hand," the place of highest honor and authority (verse 1). There he fulfills all the themes of worship in the Old Testament—priesthood, covenant, temple, and sacrifice—ministering in the liturgy of the true sanctuary created by God (verse 2). Jesus is the priest who presides at the eternal, heavenly liturgy, in which every earthly rite participates.

Since it is the role of every high priest to offer gifts and sacrifices to God, seeking atonement for sin and reconciliation between God and humanity, it is necessary that Jesus have something to offer (verse 3). While the priests of old brought lambs and bulls, grains and oils, to be sacrificed, Jesus, as we have already been told, brought the perfect sacrifice of himself. He brought an offering to God that was nothing less than the fullness of the human condition, perfected by the obedience and suffering of his entire life.

Of course this perfect, eternal sacrifice could not be contained in the tabernacle that Moses set up in the wilderness under God's instructions. This sanctuary was an elaborate tent, portable enough to be carried on the journey through the wilderness. The homilist says that this tabernacle of the exodus, a design similar to the later temple built in Jerusalem, was only "a sketch and shadow" of God's heavenly sanctuary (verse 5). God's words to Moses, "See that you make everything according to the pattern that was shown you on the mountain" (Exod 25:40), indicate that the earthly temple and its sacrificial rituals were not themselves the ultimate reality but only a prefiguring of it. Paul uses similar language when he writes about ritual aspects of the Torah: "These are only a shadow of what is to come, but the substance belongs to Christ" (Col 2:17). The earthly and temporal worship of Israel points forward to the time of Christ and upward to the heavenly realities.

The visible things of this world share in the realities of God's realm; they give us sketches and patterns of the truest realities. Yet the material world will pass away, and the highest realities will remain forever. Jesus Christ, his eternal sacrifice, and his priestly ministry for us in heaven are foreshadowed in the priesthood, sacrifices, and temple of the old covenant. As these earthly sketches fade away, we experience more deeply and personally the truest realities of God made known in Jesus.

The priestly ministry of Christ is much more excellent than that of the levitical priests, since he is the mediator of the new covenant, for which the old has prepared us (verse 6). This new covenant is based on "better promises," those assurances made through the inspired authors of old, like God's solemn oath, "You are a priest forever," and on God's pledge, given through Jeremiah, of a "new covenant" with his people, written on their hearts (Jer 31:31–33), a text to which the preacher will turn next.

Reflection and discussion
- In what sense are the rituals and liturgies of the old covenant a sketch and shadow of the fullness of new covenant worship?

- In what ways is my Sunday worship a participation in the eternal, heavenly liturgy of the high priest, Jesus Christ?

- In what ways does my understanding of Jesus as the high priest of the new covenant enrich my understanding of him?

Prayer
Eternal Priest, help me to realize that you offered the fullness of your humanity and divinity as you gave yourself in sacrifice. Help me to trust in you and receive the grace of your forgiveness for my sins.

LESSON 16   **SESSION 4**

> "They shall all know me, from the least of them to the greatest. For I will be merciful toward their iniquities, and I will remember their sins no more."
>
> HEBREWS 8:11–12

The New Covenant for God's People

HEBREWS 8:7–13 *⁷For if that first covenant had been faultless, there would have been no need to look for a second one.*

⁸God finds fault with them when he says:

"The days are surely coming, says the Lord,
    when I will establish a new covenant with the house of Israel
    and with the house of Judah;
⁹not like the covenant that I made with their ancestors,
    on the day when I took them by the hand to lead them out
        of the land of Egypt;
for they did not continue in my covenant,
    and so I had no concern for them, says the Lord.
¹⁰This is the covenant that I will make with the house of Israel
    after those days, says the Lord:
I will put my laws in their minds,
    and write them on their hearts,
and I will be their God,
    and they shall be my people.

> ¹¹*And they shall not teach one another*
>   *or say to each other, 'Know the Lord,'*
> *for they shall all know me,*
>   *from the least of them to the greatest.*
> ¹²*For I will be merciful toward their iniquities,*
>   *and I will remember their sins no more."*
>
> ¹³*In speaking of "a new covenant," he has made the first one obsolete. And what is obsolete and growing old will soon disappear.*

The preacher now turns to God's pledge, given through Jeremiah, of a "new covenant" with his people, a covenant based on the "better promises" the text offers (Jer 31:31–34). This prophecy is the one place in the Old Testament in which a new covenant is proclaimed, and the fact that this is the longest text from the Hebrew Bible quoted in the New Testament testifies to its exceptional importance for the author of Hebrews and the entire Christian tradition.

Jeremiah's prophecy was delivered at the lowest point in the history of God's people. Their continual infidelity and injustice had led to the devastation of which the prophets had continually warned. The northern kingdom of Israel had long since been conquered by the Assyrians, and now the southern kingdom of Judah had been invaded by the Babylonians, Jerusalem and its temple had been destroyed, and its king and people had been taken into exile in Babylon. Yet Jeremiah assures his hearers that God remains faithful, despite his people's long history of broken promises and sinful neglect of the covenant.

The new covenant, which the homilist proclaims has been established in the priesthood of Christ, is set in contrast with the covenant God formed with Israel at Mount Sinai after delivering his people from the slavery of Egypt (verses 8–9). Yet this new covenant is not completely different from the Sinai covenant; the essence of the relationship remains the same: "I will be their God, and they shall be my people" (verse 10). God did not revoke or annul his first covenant with Israel, as so many Christians over the centuries have tragically misinterpreted the prophecy. As Paul writes in reference to Israel, "The gifts and the calling of God are irrevocable" (Rom 11:29). The former covenant remains, but it has been outshined by the new covenant ratified by the death and resurrection of Jesus.

God finds the fault to be in the people, who seemed incapable of keeping the covenant and could never achieve its true purpose of establishing their complete and lasting unity with God. So "the days are surely coming" when God will reestablish the covenant's foundation in his Son. The new covenant will be established "with the house of Israel and with the house of Judah," symbolizing the healing of human divisions and the reconciliation of all peoples and nations in Christ. Now, through the once-for-all sacrifice of Jesus and through a faithful relationship with him, the better promises made in Jeremiah's prophecy are being fulfilled.

First, by uniting the minds and hearts of God's people with Jesus, God would implant the law within them so that they would respond faithfully through his grace. Rather than obeying ordinances "written on tablets of stone," the law would be written on the minds and hearts of those who live in Christ. Second, through a living relationship with Jesus, all would come to "know" God through an interior, direct, and immediate relationship with him (verse 11). Through faith in Christ, they would know God personally and intimately. And third, their relationship with God would come about through the divine mercy embodied in the total sacrifice of Jesus for us: "I will be merciful toward their iniquities, and I will remember their sins no more" (verse 12). In Christ, God's people could experience complete forgiveness of sins.

We live in this new covenant, in this new period of grace, with Christ as our constant mediator with God. Saying that the covenant with Israel made at Sinai is "obsolete and growing old" does not mean that God's bond of love with the Jewish people is outdated, but that the forms of worship integrally bound to that covenant will "soon disappear" (verse 13). The worship under the covenant with Moses, with it levitical priesthood, temple, and animal sacrifices, was never intended to be the permanent way of relating to God. In fact, these rituals of worship will discontinue with the destruction of Jerusalem and its temple in AD 70, perhaps shortly after Hebrews is written.

Reflection and discussion
- Do I understand my relationship with God as a covenant that involves promises and responsibilities?

- What is the main similarity between the old covenant and the new? What is the main difference between the old covenant and the new?

- What are some ways that I see the fulfillment of Jeremiah's prophecy in my own life?

Prayer
Faithful God, who taught your people to await a new covenant, you continually seek a newer and better relationship with me. I pray for the grace to know you more personally and to experience your mercy more confidently.

> He entered once for all into the Holy Place,
> not with the blood of goats and calves, but with his own blood,
> thus obtaining eternal redemption. HEBREWS 9:12

The Completeness of Christ's Sacrifice

HEBREWS 9:1–14 ¹*Now even the first covenant had regulations for worship and an earthly sanctuary.* ²*For a tent was constructed, the first one, in which were the lampstand, the table, and the bread of the Presence; this is called the Holy Place.* ³*Behind the second curtain was a tent called the Holy of Holies.* ⁴*In it stood the golden altar of incense and the ark of the covenant overlaid on all sides with gold, in which there were a golden urn holding the manna, and Aaron's rod that budded, and the tablets of the covenant;* ⁵*above it were the cherubim of glory overshadowing the mercy seat. Of these things we cannot speak now in detail.*

⁶*Such preparations having been made, the priests go continually into the first tent to carry out their ritual duties;* ⁷*but only the high priest goes into the second, and he but once a year, and not without taking the blood that he offers for himself and for the sins committed unintentionally by the people.* ⁸*By this the Holy Spirit indicates that the way into the sanctuary has not yet been disclosed as long as the first tent is still standing.* ⁹*This is a symbol of the present time, during which gifts and sacrifices are offered that cannot perfect the conscience of the worshiper,* ¹⁰*but deal only with food and drink and various baptisms, regulations for the body imposed until the time comes to set things right.*

¹¹*But when Christ came as a high priest of the good things that have come, then through the greater and perfect tent (not made with hands, that is, not of this*

creation), ¹²he entered once for all into the Holy Place, not with the blood of goats and calves, but with his own blood, thus obtaining eternal redemption. ¹³For if the blood of goats and bulls, with the sprinkling of the ashes of a heifer, sanctifies those who have been defiled so that their flesh is purified, ¹⁴how much more will the blood of Christ, who through the eternal Spirit offered himself without blemish to God, purify our conscience from dead works to worship the living God!

The homilist takes the congregation on a tour of the ancient tabernacle, based on the description scattered throughout Exodus 25—40. This sanctuary in the desert was a tent divided by curtains into two sections. Pulling back the first curtain for us, the homilist briefly describes the furnishings of the Holy Place (verse 2). Then, pulling back the second curtain, the homilist invites us to peer into the mysterious shadows of the Holy of Holies where the Ark of the Covenant resided (verses 3–5).

Yet the preacher does not want us to dwell on these furnishings. He wants us to understand the significance of the worship there so that he can compare the earthly worship in the old sanctuary with the new covenant worship through the priestly ministry of Christ. On a routine day, there are many priests in the Holy Place, busy with the activities of worship (verse 6). But on only one special day of the year, the Day of Atonement, a solitary high priest enters the Holy of Holies alone, bringing with him the blood of sacrifice, which he offers both for his own sins and those of the people (verse 7). Entrance to the Holy of Holies was thus highly restricted. Because the sanctuary was believed to be the place of God's most intimate presence, the curtain of the sanctuary was a ritual barrier that separated people from the presence of God.

The history of God's people under the earlier covenant was about waiting and hoping, reaching forward toward an experience of God they could not grasp (verses 8–10). God's people trusted in God's promises even though they did not understand precisely how those promises would be fulfilled. They worshiped God in a movable and transitory sanctuary, and they offered temporal sacrifices through an impaired priesthood. Their worship was imperfect and provisional, but it would give way to worship "in spirit and in truth" (John 4:23) made possible by the new covenant in Jesus Christ.

Our Christian worship, too, may often seem to be temporal and far less than perfect. We worship God in church buildings that may need repair; we listen to preaching that may be less than eloquent; we sing hymns that may not lift us up; we meet people who join us for a while and then move away. As God's people we long for an experience of intimacy with God, an experience in which we can personally know God's merciful forgiveness. We need someone to pull back the curtain that separates us from God and to invite us into an intimate encounter with God. The good news the preacher proclaims is that we have such a high priest in Jesus Christ. In faith we trust that wherever and whenever we gather for worship, we follow our "high priest of the good things that have come" into "the greater and perfect tent (not made with hands, that is, not of this creation)" (verse 11).

Christ is the final and perfect high priest. He has not entered into the limited presence of God in a transitory sanctuary but into God's full presence in heaven. He has entered the heavenly sanctuary not bearing the blood of animals but the blood of his own perfect sacrifice (verses 12–14). His offering obtains not a temporary purification; rather, it cleanses our consciences and obtains for us "eternal redemption." Our perfect mediator has permanently pulled back the curtain of the sanctuary that shut us off from God. Now we can enter the intimacy of God's presence and truly worship the living God.

Reflection and discussion
- What are the curtains that block my access to a deeper experience of God?

- In what ways does new covenant worship complete the sacrificial offerings of the old covenant?

- How can I experience greater intimacy with God in my public worship?

- Which aspects of my life are temporary? Which are permanent? Do I express the relative worth of each by my time and attention?

Prayer
Eternal High Priest, I know that I am a living temple of your presence. Pull back the curtains so that I may see beyond the passing aspects of this world and so that others may experience your presence through my daily life.

LESSON 18 SESSION 4

> Christ, having been offered once to bear the sins of many, will appear a second time, not to deal with sin, but to save those who are eagerly waiting for him. HEBREWS 9:28

The New Covenant Sacrifice

HEBREWS 9:15–28 ¹⁵*For this reason he is the mediator of a new covenant, so that those who are called may receive the promised eternal inheritance, because a death has occurred that redeems them from the transgressions under the first covenant.* ¹⁶*Where a will is involved, the death of the one who made it must be established.* ¹⁷*For a will takes effect only at death, since it is not in force as long as the one who made it is alive.* ¹⁸*Hence not even the first covenant was inaugurated without blood.* ¹⁹*For when every commandment had been told to all the people by Moses in accordance with the law, he took the blood of calves and goats, with water and scarlet wool and hyssop, and sprinkled both the scroll itself and all the people,* ²⁰*saying, "This is the blood of the covenant that God has ordained for you."* ²¹*And in the same way he sprinkled with the blood both the tent and all the vessels used in worship.* ²²*Indeed, under the law almost everything is purified with blood, and without the shedding of blood there is no forgiveness of sins.*

²³*Thus it was necessary for the sketches of the heavenly things to be purified with these rites, but the heavenly things themselves need better sacrifices than these.* ²⁴*For Christ did not enter a sanctuary made by human hands, a mere copy of the true one, but he entered into heaven itself, now to appear in the presence of God on our behalf.* ²⁵*Nor was it to offer himself again and again, as the high priest enters the Holy Place year after year with blood that is not his own;* ²⁶*for then he would*

have had to suffer again and again since the foundation of the world. But as it is, he has appeared once for all at the end of the age to remove sin by the sacrifice of himself. ²⁷And just as it is appointed for mortals to die once, and after that the judgment, ²⁸so Christ, having been offered once to bear the sins of many, will appear a second time, not to deal with sin, but to save those who are eagerly waiting for him.

Proclaiming Jesus Christ as "the mediator of a new covenant," the preacher goes on to explain how the inauguration of this new covenant with God requires both the death of Christ and the shedding of his blood. To explain the necessity of Christ's death, the preacher discusses the Greek word for covenant, which can also mean "will" or "testament." He explains that the covenant is like a last will and testament, which only takes effect when the person who made the will dies. The death of Jesus was necessary so that we might receive the "promised eternal inheritance." His sacrificial death is the answer to sin in every era, past and present, redeeming God's people from transgressions under the first covenant and all subsequent offenses (verses 15–17).

In order to explain the necessity for the shedding of Christ's blood, the preacher first reviews the inauguration of the covenant at Sinai. After reading the terms of the covenant, the bond was ratified by a death ritual in which Moses sacrificed animals and sprinkled their blood on the scroll, the people, the sanctuary, and the vessels of worship, proclaiming, "This is the blood of the covenant" (verses 18–21; see Exod 24:3–8). Through the shedding of blood, both parties in the covenant obligate themselves to be faithful to the stipulations of the covenant, and with the blood there is both purification and forgiveness of sin (verse 22). Because of the relational damage caused by sin, atonement for sin is costly. But rather than paying the cost with their own blood, God gave his people the rituals of sacrifice in the sanctuary. As the Torah testified, "I have given it to you for making atonement for your lives on the altar; for, as life, it is the blood that makes atonement" (Lev 17:11).

As these Old Testament rituals require both death and blood, so now the new covenant fulfills these prefigurations through the death of Jesus on the cross and the shedding of his blood. The sacrifices at Sinai, temple worship, and the annual offering by the high priest in the Holy of Holies are all "sketches" of the true heavenly worship of God. New covenant worship, for the final and comprehensive atonement for sin, requires "better sacrifices," namely, the self-offering of Christ. He offered not the blood of daily unwitting sacrifices but his own human blood, blood that is of infinite value because it was poured out in love by the incarnate Son. His suffering and saving death occurred only once for all people, the final sacrifice, perfect and complete (verses 23–26). Christ himself is the reality to which all the sketches pointed. His sacrificial work was presented in heaven itself, the transcendent dwelling place of God, and there he now continues his high priestly intercession in God's presence.

Human beings die once, and their death is followed by divine judgment (verse 27). But Christ's once-for-all death is followed by our deliverance from judgment (verse 28). As Isaiah prophesied of God's Servant, "he bore the sin of many" (Isa 53:12), so Christ was offered once "to bear the sins of many." So when Christ comes again in glory, he will appear "not to deal with sin, but to save those who are eagerly waiting for him." Those who trust in Christ's atoning work will experience redemption and the completion of God's saving plan for the world.

Reflection and discussion
- What does it mean to me that I am an heir to a promised eternal inheritance?

- What is the significance of the blood of sacrifice for both the old and new covenants?

- Why does the one sacrifice of Christ have an infinitely greater effect than the many sacrifices offered under the former covenant?

- The author uses sketches from the Old Testament to explain the meaning of Christ's death to religious Jews. How would I explain his saving death to non-religious people today?

Prayer
Lord Jesus, you gave yourself completely in love for us and poured out your priceless blood on the cross. Give me the faith to receive the gift of your perfect forgiveness of my sin and to claim the eternal inheritance you have willed for me.

SUGGESTIONS FOR FACILITATORS, GROUP SESSION 4

1. Welcome group members and ask if anyone has any questions, announcements, or requests.

2. You may want to pray this prayer as a group:
   Faithful God, who continually seeks a newer and better relationship with your people, give us the grace to know you more personally and trust in your mercy more confidently. As you established your reign in ancient Israel and through your prophets taught us to await a new covenant, give us the faith to receive the gift of your perfect forgiveness and claim the eternal inheritance you have promised. Make us living temples of your presence and unite the daily sacrifices of our lives to the cross of your Son, so that they may be pleasing offerings to you.

3. Ask one or more of the following questions:
   - What is the most difficult part of this study for you?
   - What insights stand out to you from the lessons this week?

4. Discuss lessons 13 through 18. Choose one or more of the questions for reflection and discussion from each lesson to discuss as a group. You may want to ask group members which question was most challenging or helpful to them as you review each lesson.

5. Keep the discussion moving, but allow time for the questions that provoke the most discussion. Encourage the group members to use "I" language in their responses.

6. After talking over each lesson, instruct group members to complete lessons 19 through 24 on their own during the six days before the next group meeting. They should write out their own answers to the questions as preparation for next week's session.

7. Ask the group what encouragement they need for the coming week. Ask the members to pray for the needs of one another during the week.

8. Conclude by praying aloud together the prayer at the end of one of the lessons discussed. You may choose to conclude the prayer by asking members to pray aloud any requests they may have.

LESSON 19   SESSION 5

It is by God's will that we have been sanctified through the offering of the body of Jesus Christ once for all.
HEBREWS 10:10

The Singular Self-Offering of Christ

HEBREWS 10:1–10 ¹*Since the law has only a shadow of the good things to come and not the true form of these realities, it can never, by the same sacrifices that are continually offered year after year, make perfect those who approach.* ²*Otherwise, would they not have ceased being offered, since the worshipers, cleansed once for all, would no longer have any consciousness of sin?* ³*But in these sacrifices there is a reminder of sin year after year.* ⁴*For it is impossible for the blood of bulls and goats to take away sins.* ⁵*Consequently, when Christ came into the world, he said,*

"*Sacrifices and offerings you have not desired,*
   but a body you have prepared for me;
⁶*in burnt offerings and sin offerings*
   you have taken no pleasure.
⁷*Then I said, 'See, God, I have come to do your will, O God'*
   (in the scroll of the book it is written of me)."

⁸*When he said above, "You have neither desired nor taken pleasure in sacrifices and offerings and burnt offerings and sin offerings" (these are offered according to the law),* ⁹*then he added, "See, I have come to do your will." He abolishes the first in order to establish the second.* ¹⁰*And it is by God's will that we have been sanctified through the offering of the body of Jesus Christ once for all.*

The author begins to sum up his homily on the meaning and nature of Christ's saving act. He does so by contrasting again the sacrifices of the law of Moses, which are incomplete and repetitious, with the once-for-all sacrifice of Christ, which is perfectly complete. The offerings of the former covenant are "only a shadow" of the new, unable to "make perfect those who approach" (verse 1). The many sacrifices of the old law brought a ritual and superficial cleansing to the people, but they were never able to bring about the goal of God's saving purposes for the world. They were incapable of inwardly healing the human conscience from guilt and bringing about complete forgiveness of sins. In fact, these sacrifices, especially the annual Day of Atonement, were repeated reminders of sin "year after year," which continually emphasized human guilt and unworthiness before God (verses 2–3). The fullest healing and cleansing from sin is beyond the power of the blood of animals (verse 4). Only the sacred blood of Jesus is sufficient for this saving work.

The author quotes a text from Psalm 40:6–8 in order to express why the new covenant offers us the way to receive authentic forgiveness of sins (verses 5–7). The text indicates that even the Old Testament recognizes the inadequacy of the "sacrifices and offerings and burnt offerings and sin offerings" of the levitical priesthood (verse 8). Even though they are required by the Torah, they are not what God ultimately requires. The preacher, however, wants us to read the psalm as the words of the Son speaking to God, showing us the fullest meaning of the text as fulfilled in Christ. For he is the goal of the ancient Scriptures and all is ultimately fulfilled and completed in him. In the mouth of Jesus, the psalm expresses his desire to be obedient to the will of God (verses 7, 9).

"The offering of the body of Jesus Christ once for all" is the means by which God desires humanity to be sanctified (verse 10). The obedient will of Jesus, who gave himself completely out of love for us, offering his body and shedding his blood, replaces the numerous sacrifices of old. Because of who he is for us and because of the nature of his self-offering, Jesus offers us complete forgiveness, which is interior, absolving our consciences of guilt. In Christ, we no longer have to continually try to make up for our sins, to please God with our own deeds alone. Instead, Christ has taken on all our sin and guilt, definitively reconciling humanity with God. As we accept this grace through faith and baptism, our sins are forgiven, we are born anew as God's sons and daughters, we take on the mind and heart of Christ, and we are empowered to live with the guidance of the Holy Spirit.

Reflection and discussion
- Am I weighed down by the guilt of my past sins? Do I allow myself to receive the fullness of forgiveness that God desires for me?

- In what ways did the sacrifices of old express the loving submission of the human heart? How did the sacrifice of Christ demonstrate the inadequacy of the former covenant?

- Read Psalm 51:15–17. What does God desire for the forgiveness of sins?

Prayer
Faithful God, throughout history you have been showing us the path to reconciliation with you. Work within my heart so that I can accept the inner healing, complete forgiveness, and freedom from guilt that you want so much for me.

LESSON 20 **SESSION 5**

> For by a single offering he has perfected for all time those who are sanctified. HEBREWS 10:14

The Enthroned High Priest

HEBREWS 10:11–18 ¹¹*And every priest stands day after day at his service, offering again and again the same sacrifices that can never take away sins.* ¹²*But when Christ had offered for all time a single sacrifice for sins, "he sat down at the right hand of God,"* ¹³*and since then has been waiting "until his enemies would be made a footstool for his feet."* ¹⁴*For by a single offering he has perfected for all time those who are sanctified.* ¹⁵*And the Holy Spirit also testifies to us, for after saying,*

¹⁶*"This is the covenant that I will make with them*
   after those days, says the Lord:
I will put my laws in their hearts,
   and I will write them on their minds,"
¹⁷*he also adds,*
   "I will remember their sins and their lawless deeds no more."
¹⁸*Where there is forgiveness of these, there is no longer any offering for sin.*

As the author continues to sum up his main points concerning the effects of Christ's sacrifice, he holds up two contrasting images for our reflection. The first is of many priests standing in the sanctuary, offering sacrifice every day, fruitlessly trying to bring about the forgiveness of sins for those who come to worship (verse 11). The second image is of one priest, who made one perfect offering for sins, and is now seated at the place of authority with God (verse 12). The standing priests are repeatedly trying to accomplish a task that can never be completed, whereas Christ—the one, perfect priest—is seated, having accomplished his work "for all time."

The homilist returns to one of his key texts, Psalm 110:1, but he divides the verse into two parts in order to distinguish between what Christ has accomplished—"he sat down at the right hand of God"—and what has not yet been completely achieved. Although Christ has defeated the powers of sin and death at his cross, accomplishing his victory in the world and in human lives is an ongoing process. Between Christ's sacrifice on the cross and his return in glory, he is waiting "until his enemies would be made a footstool for his feet" (verse 13). What remains is the final vindication of Christ when all the enemies of his kingdom—injustice, hatred, despair, loneliness, sickness, and grief—are fully and finally subjected to him.

The supreme value of the sacrifice of Jesus is such that "he has perfected for all time those who are sanctified" (verse 14). Because Christ's sacrifice has completed God's saving purposes among his people, its effects last forever, in contrast to the temporary effects of the many levitical sacrifices. Those who are being made holy through his self-offering are moving toward the fullness of salvation promised and foreshadowed by all that preceded in the covenant on Sinai.

The homilist returns to his most crucial text to drive home his point, quoting again the "new covenant" passage of Jeremiah. The Holy Spirit is considered the ultimate inspiration for all the Scriptures, creating a living word that speaks to every age, and thus the Spirit testifies to us through the prophet's words (verse 15). Dividing the text into two parts, the author first spotlights the promise of the new covenant and its internal effects within God's people (verse 16). Then he arrives at the climax of his preaching with the final verse: "I will remember their sins and their lawless deeds no more" (verse 17). This is the kind of forgiveness that people truly need. Not only does God wipe away our sins; he blots them out of the divine memory. So complete is God's merciful forgiveness of our sins that there is no reason to experience the burden of guilt. For this reason, the many offerings of the former covenant are no longer significant when we experience God's perfect forgiveness through Jesus Christ (verse 18).

Reflection and discussion

- What are the main similarities and differences between the two images in verses 11–12?

- What are the enemies of Christ in my life that still need to be put under Christ's feet?

- Do I trust in Christ's forgiveness enough to know that he does not remember my past sins?

Prayer

Merciful priest of the new covenant, let me trust in your words: "I will remember their sins and their lawless deeds no more." Show me that your forgiveness is perfect and that you are healing my conscience of guilt and shame.

LESSON 21 SESSION 5

> Let us approach with a true heart in full assurance of faith, with our hearts sprinkled clean from an evil conscience and our bodies washed with pure water. HEBREWS 10:22

Call to Worship, Faith, and Perseverance

HEBREWS 10:19–39 ¹⁹Therefore, my friends, since we have confidence to enter the sanctuary by the blood of Jesus, ²⁰by the new and living way that he opened for us through the curtain (that is, through his flesh), ²¹and since we have a great priest over the house of God, ²²let us approach with a true heart in full assurance of faith, with our hearts sprinkled clean from an evil conscience and our bodies washed with pure water. ²³Let us hold fast to the confession of our hope without wavering, for he who has promised is faithful. ²⁴And let us consider how to provoke one another to love and good deeds, ²⁵not neglecting to meet together, as is the habit of some, but encouraging one another, and all the more as you see the Day approaching.

²⁶For if we willfully persist in sin after having received the knowledge of the truth, there no longer remains a sacrifice for sins, ²⁷but a fearful prospect of judgment, and a fury of fire that will consume the adversaries. ²⁸Anyone who has violated the law of Moses dies without mercy "on the testimony of two or three witnesses." ²⁹How much worse punishment do you think will be deserved by those who have spurned the Son of God, profaned the blood of the covenant by which they were sanctified, and outraged the Spirit of grace? ³⁰For we know the one who said, "Vengeance is mine, I will repay." And again, "The Lord will judge his people." ³¹It is a fearful thing to fall into the hands of the living God.

³²But recall those earlier days when, after you had been enlightened, you endured a hard struggle with sufferings, ³³sometimes being publicly exposed to abuse and persecution, and sometimes being partners with those so treated. ³⁴For you had compassion for those who were in prison, and you cheerfully accepted the plundering of your possessions, knowing that you yourselves possessed something better and more lasting. ³⁵Do not, therefore, abandon that confidence of yours; it brings a great reward. ³⁶For you need endurance, so that when you have done the will of God, you may receive what was promised. ³⁷For yet

"*in a very little while,*

    the one who is coming will come and will not delay;
³⁸but my righteous one will live by faith.

    My soul takes no pleasure in anyone who shrinks back."
³⁹But we are not among those who shrink back and so are lost, but among those who have faith and so are saved.

Having delivered his climactic presentation on the priesthood of Christ, the preacher now draws out the practical applications of his teaching for the community. He begins with "therefore," thus letting us know that he is about to answer the questions that every member of the congregation asks of a sermon: "So what now?" "What am I to do about this?" "How do I practically respond?"

Before issuing a series of exhortations to his listeners, the author pulls together several themes from his teaching to remind his listeners of the reasons they can respond with confidence (verses 19–21). Christ is our great priest who has parted the curtain that separated humanity from God. What had previously been the privilege of the high priest one day in the year is now the privilege of every member of the community of faith. Through his flesh and his blood, Christ has opened our way into the heavenly sanctuary of God's presence so that we can approach God with absolute trust.

The first of the author's exhortations implores us to confidently draw near to God in worship and prayer (verse 22). Because we have been truly forgiven, no longer burdened by a guilty conscience, and because we are now interiorly clean through baptismal waters, we can come close to God and personally experience God's divine life.

The second exhortation entreats us to hold unwaveringly to our faith in Jesus and to the hope he gives us (verse 23). God has given us promises throughout salvation history and has fulfilled those promises in Christ. Though it is easy to give up or to grow disheartened in the midst of struggle, we know that we can trust Jesus.

The third exhortation pleads us to rouse one another to love and to the good works that come from love (verse 24). We must come to the communal Eucharist to take part in sacramental worship and encourage others to do so as well (verse 25). New covenant worship joins us not only to God in Christ but to one another.

After exhorting his listeners with confidence, the homilist's mood becomes grim. His pastoral judgment indicates that stern warnings are also necessary to support the waning faith of his audience. "If we willfully persist in sin," he cautions, while knowing the truth revealed to us in Christ, we risk the grace of salvation (verses 26–27). By willfully refusing the mercy of God made known in Christ's sacrifice, we face the prospect of God's judgment and the divine wrath. The sin described here is apostasy—the informed, deliberate rejection of the gospel of Christ by one who has previously experienced its forgiveness and grace. By refusing the salvation God offers, we cut ourselves off from the grace that God freely and continually offers us. Of course, since only God can know the deepest intentions of another person's heart, this is a deadly sin that only God can judge.

It seems that the community being addressed had become complacent and begun to lose heart. Their situation was increasingly urgent, and they were in danger of abandoning the gospel. To warn them even more forcefully, the homilist compares judgment for offenses under the former covenant and the new. If disobedience to the law of Moses was so serious that an offender was put to death without mercy, how much more fearful must be the consequences for rejecting the saving work of Christ (verses 28–29). For our God is not an inert idol but "the living God," who sees into the depths of the human heart and holds his creatures accountable (verse 31).

As a skilled pastor, the homilist moves from warnings of God's vengeance back to reassuring advice, for his goal is not to generate fear but encouragement during the present crisis. He does so by asking the congregation to recall their earlier enthusiasm and commitment to the gospel. In those days, their experiences of affliction, persecution, imprisonment, and confiscation of property only deepened their understanding of the imperishable nature of the gospel (verses 32–34). If they persevered in the past, then they can endure their struggles in the present and in the future, whatever it may hold. They must maintain their confident hope, trusting in God's promises (verses 35–36). The words of the prophet Habakkuk (Hab 2:3–4, Greek version) stir the listeners to live faithfully lest they fall away in a time of tribulation (verses 37–39). They must not shrink back and be lost but have faith and be saved.

Reflection and discussion
- Which of these exhortations do I need to hear most today?

- What can I do practically to approach God with greater confidence?

- What memories from the earlier period of my life in Christ can bring me confidence and encouragement in my present struggles?

Prayer
Faithful God, in the midst of struggles and discouragement, help me to trust your word about Jesus and his priesthood. I want to worship you with confidence, to hope in your promises, and to encourage my brothers and sisters in the faith we share.

LESSON 22  **SESSION 5**

Without faith it is impossible to please God, for whoever would approach him must believe that he exists and that he rewards those who seek him. HEBREWS 11:6

Examples of Faith

HEBREWS 11:1–7 ¹*Now faith is the assurance of things hoped for, the conviction of things not seen.* ²*Indeed, by faith our ancestors received approval.* ³*By faith we understand that the worlds were prepared by the word of God, so that what is seen was made from things that are not visible.*

⁴*By faith Abel offered to God a more acceptable sacrifice than Cain's. Through this he received approval as righteous, God himself giving approval to his gifts; he died, but through his faith he still speaks.* ⁵*By faith Enoch was taken so that he did not experience death; and "he was not found, because God had taken him." For it was attested before he was taken away that "he had pleased God."* ⁶*And without faith it is impossible to please God, for whoever would approach him must believe that he exists and that he rewards those who seek him.* ⁷*By faith Noah, warned by God about events as yet unseen, respected the warning and built an ark to save his household; by this he condemned the world and became an heir to the righteousness that is in accordance with faith.*

The author began the homily with these words: "Long ago God spoke to our ancestors in many and various ways" (1:1); now, in this chapter, the homilist shows how in many and various ways our ancestors responded to God in faith. He offers us a chronicle of the heroes of God's former covenant with Israel, told from the point of view of their faith in God and in the promises God offered them. These ancestors still guide us, giving us encouragement and strength in our struggles. Like the stained-glass figures that surround us in Christian worship, these models of faith inspire us by their example and summon us to continue in the way they have set before us.

Setting the theme, the author begins by offering us a description of faith (verse 1). This is not a dogmatic definition meant to include all aspects of faith. It is, rather, a homiletic description meant to highlight those aspects of faith the author wants to encourage. Faith is, first, "the assurance of things hoped for," a kind of inward guarantee that God can be trusted. It is confidence that the future will indeed be as God has promised. Faith is also "the conviction of things not seen." It is the certainty that what cannot be seen or grasped is nonetheless real. In addressing the Corinthians Paul says, "What can be seen is temporary, but what cannot be seen is eternal" (2 Cor 4:18). Later he adds, "We walk by faith, not by sight" (2 Cor 5:7). As the fox says to the little boy in Saint-Exupery's story *The Little Prince*, "It is only with the heart that one can see rightly; what is essential is invisible to the eye."

The previously quoted words of Habakkuk, "My righteous one will live by faith" (Heb 10:38), encouraged the listeners to live with faith lest they fall away in the midst of trial. Now we are shown what faith looks like with these real-life examples to imitate. Each shows that faith is not a passive belief but an active, dynamic faithfulness, an allegiance to God especially in tribulation. These ancestors who lived by faith were so convinced of God's truthfulness that they staked their whole life on his promises. Because they took God at his word and lived their lives accordingly, their lives received divine "approval" and now serve as examples to their descendants (verse 2).

The biblical chronicle begins with creation itself. The universe of space and time was fashioned by "the word of God," as the beginning of Genesis recounts. Visible reality came forth from the invisible; "what is seen was made from things that are not visible" (verse 3). Belief that creation is divinely willed and therefore totally dependent on God for its existence is the foundation of all other acts of faith.

The first three champions of faith are drawn from the earliest chapters of Genesis. Abel, Enoch, and Noah were motivated by the unseen reality of God and his purposes as they responded with obedient faithfulness. Abel's offering was acceptable to God because he offered his best to God and held nothing back, whereas Cain in some way held back from God and kept the best for himself (verse 4). Although Abel was killed by his brother, Abel's example sheds light on the meaning of faith, and his faithfulness still speaks to his descendants. Enoch is a mysterious figure who was taken to God's heavenly realm without experiencing death because "he had pleased God" (verses 5–6). Since "without faith it is impossible to please God," Enoch serves as an example of faith because his life was spent in trust and seeking the unseen God. Noah, too, lived by faith, trusting in God's word when warned about things not yet seen (verse 7). The faith of Noah contrasted with the unbelief and corruption of the world, and he became a model of faith that expresses itself in action.

Reflection and discussion

- Do I have the kind of faith described in verse 1? In what aspects of life is my faith weak? Where is my faith strong?

- In what ways does faith in God as creator both complement and elevate the knowledge of the world we gain from human reason and science?

- In what ways might the lives of Abel, Enoch, and Noah prefigure the life of Jesus?

Prayer
God of covenant promises, you assured our ancestors of your truthfulness and asked them to respond in faithfulness. Strengthen me so that I will not become slack in following your will, and give me the confidence I need to persevere.

LESSON 23 SESSION 5

All of these died in faith without having received the promises, but from a distance they saw and greeted them.
HEBREWS 11:13

Israel's Ancestors Lived by Faith

HEBREWS 11:8–22 *⁸By faith Abraham obeyed when he was called to set out for a place that he was to receive as an inheritance; and he set out, not knowing where he was going. ⁹By faith he stayed for a time in the land he had been promised, as in a foreign land, living in tents, as did Isaac and Jacob, who were heirs with him of the same promise. ¹⁰For he looked forward to the city that has foundations, whose architect and builder is God. ¹¹By faith he received power of procreation, even though he was too old—and Sarah herself was barren—because he considered him faithful who had promised. ¹²Therefore from one person, and this one as good as dead, descendants were born, "as many as the stars of heaven and as the innumerable grains of sand by the seashore."*

¹³All of these died in faith without having received the promises, but from a distance they saw and greeted them. They confessed that they were strangers and foreigners on the earth, ¹⁴for people who speak in this way make it clear that they are seeking a homeland. ¹⁵If they had been thinking of the land that they had left behind, they would have had opportunity to return. ¹⁶But as it is, they desire a better country, that is, a heavenly one. Therefore God is not ashamed to be called their God; indeed, he has prepared a city for them.

¹⁷By faith Abraham, when put to the test, offered up Isaac. He who had received the promises was ready to offer up his only son, ¹⁸of whom he had been told, "It is through Isaac that descendants shall be named for you." ¹⁹He considered the fact that God is able even to raise someone from the dead—and figuratively speaking, he did receive him back. ²⁰By faith Isaac invoked blessings for the future on Jacob and Esau. ²¹By faith Jacob, when dying, blessed each of the sons of Joseph, "bowing in worship over the top of his staff." ²²By faith Joseph, at the end of his life, made mention of the exodus of the Israelites and gave instructions about his burial.

The longest section of this chronicle of biblical models is devoted to Abraham, the father of the people of Israel. Above all his many qualities, he is best known for his faith. Paul described Abraham as "the ancestor of all who believe" (Rom 4:11). The author of Hebrews holds up the life of Abraham as a model of faith, highlighting three major chapters in his life.

First of all, Abraham was sent by God on a journey of faith. He obeyed and departed, not knowing where he was going, trusting only that God would give him the land as an inheritance (verse 8). He left the known and familiar, entrusting his future to God. Reaching the land he had been promised, Abraham continued to journey in tents, like a stranger in a foreign land (verse 9). A man of faith, Abraham was utterly dependent on God and motivated only by God's promises.

The second illustration of Abraham's faith is his trusting belief in God's promises of descendants. Abraham was promised what was humanly impossible. Though he was old and Sarah was barren, God promised Abraham that they would have descendants in abundance (verses 11–12). Abraham and Sarah received the power of procreation because they trusted in the faithfulness and trustworthiness of God.

The last example of Abraham's faith was the testing involved in the offering of his son Isaac. Abraham's faith was so strong that "he considered the fact that God is able even to raise someone from the dead" (verses 17–19). God's act of saving Isaac from death was as though God had raised him from the dead. Yet the allusion goes beyond Isaac to the anticipation of Christ. Like Abraham, God willingly offered his only Son; then he lifted him from death in the resurrection. Belief in the power of God to raise the dead to life is the greatest faith.

The chapters of Abraham's life demonstrate the faith described by the homilist: "Faith is the assurance of things hoped for, the conviction of things not seen" (11:1). Abraham was the original pilgrim—journeying toward the unseen and unknown, acting on the basis of God's promises alone. The things hoped for guided his life, though he died without having received the promises (verse 13). He spent his life reaching for what he only glimpsed in the distance.

The promises and blessings experienced by Abraham, as wonderful as they were, were only a shadow of the transcendent reality still to come. Like all of us, he knew that his true "homeland" was not to be found in his earthly life (verse 14). The promised land was only a tract of real estate on the eastern shore of the Mediterranean. Abraham looked forward to "a better country" (verse 16), to "the city that has foundations," a stable and lasting city "whose architect and builder is God" (verse 10).

Abraham's faith was not a passive waiting; it was a lively obedience and active pilgrimage motivated by God's trustworthiness. God's promises, the things hoped for, though not yet seen, are a powerful motivator for people of faith. This sense of incompletion runs throughout the stories of our Old Testament ancestors. Each generation passed on those promises to the next: Isaac, when he was near death, to his sons Jacob and Esau (verse 20); and Jacob, when his life was fading, to his grandsons (verse 21). Joseph, at the end of his life, was given a glimpse of the exodus, and in faith he gave instructions that his bones should be brought into the land of God's promises (verse 22).

Like Abraham, we live our lives as traveling pilgrims, not always knowing where we are going but led by God's promises. The journey is never confined to one generation, it is in opposition to our culture that wants everything now, and it is always challenging and risky. Faith does not tell us when or where or how God will fulfill promises, but it assures us that God will indeed fulfill our hopes.

Reflection and discussion
- What obstacles did Abraham have to overcome in each of the three episodes that illustrate his faith?

- What three chapters of my life have best demonstrated the challenges of faith?

- In what ways is Abraham a model of faith for me?

Prayer
God of our ancestors, you have called us to be traveling pilgrims on the earth and have assured us that you are faithful to your promises. May we join with all the sons and daughters of Abraham as we journey together toward our final homeland with you.

LESSON 24   SESSION 5

God had provided something better so that they would not, apart from us, be made perfect. HEBREWS 11:40

All Were Waiting for God's Promise

HEBREWS 11:23–40 ²³*By faith Moses was hidden by his parents for three months after his birth, because they saw that the child was beautiful; and they were not afraid of the king's edict.* ²⁴*By faith Moses, when he was grown up, refused to be called a son of Pharaoh's daughter,* ²⁵*choosing rather to share ill-treatment with the people of God than to enjoy the fleeting pleasures of sin.* ²⁶*He considered abuse suffered for the Christ to be greater wealth than the treasures of Egypt, for he was looking ahead to the reward.* ²⁷*By faith he left Egypt, unafraid of the king's anger; for he persevered as though he saw him who is invisible.* ²⁸*By faith he kept the Passover and the sprinkling of blood, so that the destroyer of the firstborn would not touch the firstborn of Israel.*

²⁹*By faith the people passed through the Red Sea as if it were dry land, but when the Egyptians attempted to do so they were drowned.* ³⁰*By faith the walls of Jericho fell after they had been encircled for seven days.* ³¹*By faith Rahab the prostitute did not perish with those who were disobedient, because she had received the spies in peace.*

³²*And what more should I say? For time would fail me to tell of Gideon, Barak, Samson, Jephthah, of David and Samuel and the prophets—* ³³*who through faith conquered kingdoms, administered justice, obtained promises, shut the mouths of lions,* ³⁴*quenched raging fire, escaped the edge of the sword, won strength out of weakness, became mighty in war, put foreign armies to flight.* ³⁵*Women received*

their dead by resurrection. Others were tortured, refusing to accept release, in order to obtain a better resurrection. ³⁶Others suffered mocking and flogging, and even chains and imprisonment. ³⁷They were stoned to death, they were sawn in two, they were killed by the sword; they went about in skins of sheep and goats, destitute, persecuted, tormented— ³⁸of whom the world was not worthy. They wandered in deserts and mountains, and in caves and holes in the ground.

³⁹Yet all these, though they were commended for their faith, did not receive what was promised, ⁴⁰since God had provided something better so that they would not, apart from us, be made perfect.

The preacher continues to evoke a long list of men and women to serve as models of faith and perseverance under great difficulty. Some of them are familiar to us, like Abraham, Sarah, Moses, and David. Some might not be so familiar, like Rahab, Gideon, Barak, and Jephthah. But the chronicle encourages us to turn to the ancient Scriptures in order to learn the stories of our ancestors in faith. Like the Christian communion of saints, they inspire us and support us in our journey through life.

Moses assumes a major place in the chronicle as episodes from his heroic life are recounted with the continual refrain, "by faith." His survival as a newborn depended on the faith of his parents as they hid their child from the genocidal orders of the pharaoh (verse 23). When Moses was given the choice to remain in the royal family of the pharaoh or to join his own suffering people, he chose his true identity (verses 24–25). Through solidarity with God's own people, he intuited that his own sufferings would somehow lead to the reward of their future Messiah (verse 26). Unafraid of the pharaoh, Moses led his people out of Egypt under the guidance of the invisible God and obediently following the ritual of Passover to save the firstborn of his people (verses 27–28).

The people exhibited the same faith as Moses as they passed through the parted waters of the sea and left the bondage of their captors (verse 29). As they entered the promised land, they trustingly circled the walls of Jericho as God gave them victory (verse 30). But Rahab, the prostitute who had previously saved the Israelite spies by hiding them in her home, was rescued because she had trusted in the unseen promises of God (verse 31).

The pace of the sermon quickens, and the preaching reaches its climax in these final verses (verses 32–38). The details of the earlier examples give way to a quickening roll call of faithful ones who endured through suffering. Some of the references are clear to us; others are quite obscure. All the phrases tell of people before the time of Christ whose faith was tested and purified through terrible suffering. Apart from faith, suffering seems to be meaningless, yet joined with a faithful anticipation of God's promises, trials unite God's people with a sense of encouraging solidarity. Intertwined with faith, suffering can till our hard ground into the fertile soil of compassion and hope. The author is helping his listeners choose the challenging struggles of the life of faith rather than an easier way of life.

Finally, the homilist pauses as the preaching reaches its peak. "Yet," he says slowly, "all these, though they were commended for their faith, did not receive what was promised" (verse 39). Despite all that suffering, all that travel, all that endurance, all that faith, they did not experience the ultimate goal. Why? Because God wanted to give us "something better," which is Jesus Christ and all the blessings of the new covenant (verse 40). Without his priesthood, his sacrifice, his inheritance, and his promises, neither we nor our ancestors could be "made perfect," that is, share in the fullness of life God desires for all people.

Reflection and discussion
- What does the example of Moses teach me about the life of faith?

- In what sense is suffering sanctified by faith?

- How are suffering and faith intertwined in my life? How has suffering given me better vision, solidarity, or hope?

- What figures from the New Testament or saints of the church could I add to this list of faithful ancestors?

Prayer
Wounded Lord, the faith of your people is purified through trial, struggle, and endurance. Help me to accept suffering, to sanctify my suffering with faith, and to see beyond suffering to the life you have promised.

SUGGESTIONS FOR FACILITATORS, GROUP SESSION 5

1. Welcome group members and ask if anyone has any questions, announcements, or requests.

2. You may want to pray this prayer as a group:
   God of covenant promises, you assured our ancestors of your truthfulness and asked them to respond in faithfulness. We want to worship you with confidence, hope in your promises, and encourage one another in the faith we share. Strengthen us so that we will not become slack in following your will, and give us the assurance we need to persevere. Work within our hearts so that we can accept the inner healing, complete forgiveness, and freedom from guilt that you want so much for us.

3. Ask one or more of the following questions:
   - What most intrigued you from this week's study?
   - What makes you want to know and understand more of God's word?

4. Discuss lessons 19 through 24. Choose one or more of the questions for reflection and discussion from each lesson to talk over as a group.

5. Ask the group members to name one thing they have most appreciated about the way the group has worked during this Bible study. Ask group members to discuss any changes they might suggest in the way the group works in future studies.

6. Invite group members to complete lessons 25 through 30 on their own during the six days before the next meeting. They should write out their own answers to the questions as preparation for next week's session.

7. Ask group members to name ways that their study of Hebrews helped them understand the meaning of worship in the new covenant. Discuss some of these insights.

8. Conclude by praying aloud together the prayer at the end of one of the lessons discussed. You may want to conclude the prayer by asking members to voice prayers of thanksgiving.

LESSON 25 SESSION 6

Discipline always seems painful rather than pleasant at the time, but later it yields the peaceful fruit of righteousness to those who have been trained by it.
HEBREWS 12:11

Jesus the Pioneer and Perfecter of Faith

HEBREWS 12:1–11 ¹*Therefore, since we are surrounded by so great a cloud of witnesses, let us also lay aside every weight and the sin that clings so closely, and let us run with perseverance the race that is set before us, ²looking to Jesus the pioneer and perfecter of our faith, who for the sake of the joy that was set before him endured the cross, disregarding its shame, and has taken his seat at the right hand of the throne of God.*

³Consider him who endured such hostility against himself from sinners, so that you may not grow weary or lose heart. ⁴In your struggle against sin you have not yet resisted to the point of shedding your blood. ⁵And you have forgotten the exhortation that addresses you as children—

"My child, do not regard lightly the discipline of the Lord,
  or lose heart when you are punished by him;
⁶for the Lord disciplines those whom he loves,
  and chastises every child whom he accepts."

⁷Endure trials for the sake of discipline. God is treating you as children; for what child is there whom a parent does not discipline? ⁸If you do not have that discipline in which all children share, then you are illegitimate and not his children. ⁹Moreover, we had human parents to discipline us, and we respected them. Should we not be even more willing to be subject to the Father of spirits and live? ¹⁰For they disciplined us for a short time as seemed best to them, but he disciplines us for our good, in order that we may share his holiness. ¹¹Now, discipline always seems painful rather than pleasant at the time, but later it yields the peaceful fruit of righteousness to those who have been trained by it.

Evoking the image of running the race, the homilist exhorts, "Let us run with perseverance." Since we have the inspiration of so many who have run the race before us, he urges us to run toward the goal. But in order to persevere, we must remove everything that hinders us—"every weight and the sin that clings so closely" (verse 1). We have around us the "cloud of witnesses," the heroes of the Old Testament, who are now our cheering audience in the athletic stadium of the Christian life. They have already run the race to give us strength, yet they did not reach the finish line. They are now depending on us to complete the race, so that all may experience the promised rewards.

Following the author's chronicle of the ancestors, he has saved the perfect example of faith to last. Jesus is "the pioneer and perfecter of our faith" (verse 2). As his priesthood surpassed and completed the priesthood of old, so his faithfulness exceeded and perfected that of the ancestors. As he endured the cross, so we must withstand the race. Despite the pain, Jesus fixed his eyes on the "joy that was set before him," trusting that he would reach the goal of faith and inherit God's promises. He was the first to run the race of faith to its goal. He shows us not only how to run like our ancestors but how to reach the finish line.

Consideration of the trials Jesus endured—the opposition of sinners, the shame of the cross, and the shedding of his blood—will help the community to withstand the race, struggle against sin, and not lose heart (verses 3–4). Attempting to show suffering in a positive light, the author quotes Proverbs 3:11–12. Like a good parent, the Lord disciplines his children out of love for them (verses 5–7). The trials the community endures should be understood not only as God's loving discipline but also as a sure indication that they are truly God's children (verse 8).

Just as we accepted the chastisement of our earthly parents without questioning their authority or losing respect for them, we should be even more submissive to the discipline of our spiritual Father in heaven (verse 9). As we were reprimanded during our childhood according to the best subjective judgments of our parents, God disciplines us throughout our life in according with his own knowledge of what is good for us, with the final goal "that we may share his holiness" (verse 10). By connecting the trials of life with the pursuit of holiness, the author show how these struggles have an essential purpose in the formation of God's children.

Although trials seem to produce pain at the time they are being experienced, their results are "the peaceful fruit of righteousness" (verse 11). Usually the ability to see the peaceful fruits of this loving discipline comes only by looking backward with the perspective of time. In running the race, those who have been "trained" through discipline are the ones whose joints and muscles are up to the challenge. Although suffering is necessary for the life of faith, it leads to the victorious goal and the unimaginable joy of sharing in divine life.

Reflection and discussion
- What excessive weight, burdens, or sins must I get rid of in order to run the race to the finish line?

- How close to the finish line am I in the stadium of Christian life? What does Jesus have to teach me as my mentor and coach?

- How does the perspective of discipline and training help me to understand my trials in a new way?

- What experience of suffering has God used to help me share in his holiness?

Prayer
Divine master, though I get weary and frustrated, give me the strength to endure the struggles of the race. Help me to understand your purpose in making me holy, and keep my vision focused on your goal for my life.

LESSON 26  **SESSION 6**

Lift your drooping hands and strengthen your weak knees,
and make straight paths for your feet.
HEBREWS 12:12–13

Let No One Fail to Obtain God's Grace

HEBREWS 12:12–17 ¹²Therefore lift your drooping hands and strengthen your weak knees, ¹³and make straight paths for your feet, so that what is lame may not be put out of joint, but rather be healed.
¹⁴Pursue peace with everyone, and the holiness without which no one will see the Lord. ¹⁵See to it that no one fails to obtain the grace of God; that no root of bitterness springs up and causes trouble, and through it many become defiled. ¹⁶See to it that no one becomes like Esau, an immoral and godless person, who sold his birthright for a single meal. ¹⁷You know that later, when he wanted to inherit the blessing, he was rejected, for he found no chance to repent, even though he sought the blessing with tears.

Like a coach urging on the team of runners, the preacher rallies his listeners as they continue the race. "Lift your drooping hands and strengthen your weak knees" are the words of Isaiah 35:3, in which the prophet cheers on those who are weary and discouraged by their sufferings in exile (verse 12). For both Isaiah and our preacher, what enables God's people to summon their energies and hasten forward is confident hope in God's promises.

"Make straight paths for your feet" are the words of Proverbs 4:26, a parent's instruction to keep on the right path: Keep your eyes forward and your gaze straight ahead, your feet straight on the path, not swerving to the right or the left (verse 13). With these words, the preacher exhorts those running the race to avoid weaving or wavering but to keep moving directly toward the goal. As God has promised to heal the lame, he will restore the weak and vulnerable so that they can reach the finish line.

The runners in the author's metaphorical race must be concerned not just with themselves and their own reward; they have a responsibility for one another (verse 14). Two of the primary attributes of Christian community that all must pursue together are "peace" and "holiness." Both of these aspects of the divine life remind the hearers that we progress toward the goal of life not as isolated individuals but as a community. We must watch over one another and help each other reach the finish line.

Because we are in the race together, we must make sure "that no one fails to obtain the grace of God," gives up, and drops out of the race (verse 15). The lapse of one member of the community will have inevitable effects on others. Like a "root of bitterness" that can grow and defile those around it, even one person whose heart has become bitter can poison others and have a devastating effect on a community.

The author underlines the danger of anyone failing to obtain God's grace and becoming a bitter root in the community by bringing up the counterexample of Esau (verses 16–17), whose life strongly contrasts with the heroes of faith in the previous chapter. Esau illustrates how easy it is to stray from the faith for a life that is more instantly satisfying. Esau passed up his father's blessing because he was hungry for a meal, so he lost the inheritance that was his right as the firstborn. Unlike the heroes of faith, he traded what is unseen and that lies in the future for immediate gratification in the present. Of course, Esau bitterly regretted his choice, but he was unable to repent and gain back his inheritance. Through Esau, we are reminded again about how serious apostasy is and how difficult repentance is for anyone who abandons the faith.

Reflection and discussion
- Am I better at sprints or long-distance races? What fuels me for the race?

- How can I both run the race and encourage those around me?

- What is the benefit of delayed gratification in the Christian life?

Prayer
Lord Jesus, who was the first to run the race to its goal, show us how to maintain our strength and stamina. May we support and encourage one another as we all look toward the reward God has promised us.

LESSON 27   SESSION 6

> Since we are receiving a kingdom that cannot be shaken,
> let us give thanks, by which we offer to God an
> acceptable worship with reverence and awe.
> HEBREWS 12:28

The Earthly Sinai and the Heavenly Zion

HEBREWS 12:18–29 ¹⁸*You have not come to something that can be touched, a blazing fire, and darkness, and gloom, and a tempest,* ¹⁹*and the sound of a trumpet, and a voice whose words made the hearers beg that not another word be spoken to them.* ²⁰*(For they could not endure the order that was given, "If even an animal touches the mountain, it shall be stoned to death."* ²¹*Indeed, so terrifying was the sight that Moses said, "I tremble with fear.")* ²²*But you have come to Mount Zion and to the city of the living God, the heavenly Jerusalem, and to innumerable angels in festal gathering,* ²³*and to the assembly of the firstborn who are enrolled in heaven, and to God the judge of all, and to the spirits of the righteous made perfect,* ²⁴*and to Jesus, the mediator of a new covenant, and to the sprinkled blood that speaks a better word than the blood of Abel.*

²⁵*See that you do not refuse the one who is speaking; for if they did not escape when they refused the one who warned them on earth, how much less will we escape if we reject the one who warns from heaven!* ²⁶*At that time his voice shook the earth; but now he has promised, "Yet once more I will shake not only the earth but also the heaven."* ²⁷*This phrase, "Yet once more," indicates the removal of what is shaken—that is, created things—so that what cannot be shaken may remain.* ²⁸*Therefore, since we are receiving a kingdom that cannot be shaken, let us give*

thanks, by which we offer to God an acceptable worship with reverence and awe; ^{29}*for indeed our God is a consuming fire.*

Two contrasting scenes are placed before the imagination of the hearers: God's covenant with Moses, represented by Mount Sinai, and the new covenant in Jesus Christ, represented by Mount Zion. The former covenant is depicted with fire, darkness, storm, and quaking—tangible images derived from the wilderness accounts of Exodus and Deuteronomy (verses 18–21). They also heard the blast of a trumpet and the divine voice that sounded so frightening that the people begged not to hear it. The majestic holiness of God seemed so unapproachable that even an animal was to be stoned if it touched the mountain, and the scene was so terrifying that even Moses trembled with fear.

But the congregation has not arrived at fearful Sinai. Rather, we have approached Mount Zion, "the city of the living God, the heavenly Jerusalem" (verse 22). Here we can confidently approach the throne of God, where we experience joy and celebration. Here we are with countless angels and with "the assembly of the firstborn"—the gathering before God of those who are baptized in Christ and therefore "enrolled in heaven" (verse 23). And, most important, in this heavenly city we are with Jesus, "the mediator of a new covenant" (verse 24). Through his sprinkled blood, the once-for-all atoning sacrifice for sin, God is worshiped in heaven always. Unlike Mount Sinai where the blood of Abel cries out continually for reconciliation, Mount Zion is a place where guilt may be left outside the gates and where the redeemed may experience the goal of God's saving will.

Of course, the God of Mount Sinai and Mount Zion is one and the same God, but at Sinai God approached his unsanctified people, and at Zion God encounters his people redeemed in Christ. The voice of the same God speaks: "the one who warned them on earth" at Sinai is "the one who warns from heaven" (verse 25). If the people who refused to heed God's will in the wilderness did not escape God's judgment, then those who turn away from the divine revelation of the new covenant will experience a proportionally greater judgment. The greater the light, the more serious is its rejection.

The author quotes the prophet Haggai to refer to God's impending judgment: "Yet once more I will shake not only the earth but also the heaven" (verse 27; see Hag 2:6, 21). The preacher's congregation would soon (in AD 70) experience the destruction of the earthly Jerusalem, watch its temple be reduced to rubble, and witness the end of its levitical priesthood and material sacrifices. What will remain is "a kingdom that cannot be shaken," the reign of God brought about by God's reconciling grace in Christ (verse 28).

For Christians, this coming kingdom is not a cause for fear but for confidence and joyful hope. It is already present, especially in the new covenant worship of the church. Through the thankful praise of God's children, "we offer to God an acceptable worship with reverence and awe." God is still "a consuming fire," a description of the divine presence offered by Moses to exhort God's people to faithfulness to the covenant (verse 29; see Deut 4:24; 9:3). But now we are able to stand in the presence of that divine fire and know that it is the fire of God's blazing love. Our new covenant worship is the eternal intercession of Christ through which we receive the grace of his sacrifice as we adore our God with thankfulness, reverence, and awe.

Reflection and discussion
- In what ways does the author's presentations of Mount Sinai and Mount Zion summarize many of the claims of the previous chapters?

- Why is it significant that the God revealed at Mount Sinai is the same God revealed at Mount Zion?

- How is the Christian Eucharist a participation in the divine worship of the new covenant?

- How are the words of Moses, "Our God is a consuming fire," understood differently in the assembly of the new covenant?

Prayer
God of Sinai and Zion, you invite your people to worship you with gratitude, reverence, and awe. May the fire of your love refine and purify me so that I can join my life to the sacrifice of Jesus as a holy offering to you.

LESSON 28   **SESSION 6**

> Remember your leaders, those who spoke the word of God to you;
> consider the outcome of their way of life, and imitate their faith.
> HEBREWS 13:7

Encouragement to Live a Transformed Life

HEBREWS 13:1–8 ¹*Let mutual love continue.* ²*Do not neglect to show hospitality to strangers, for by doing that some have entertained angels without knowing it.* ³*Remember those who are in prison, as though you were in prison with them; those who are being tortured, as though you yourselves were being tortured.* ⁴*Let marriage be held in honor by all, and let the marriage bed be kept undefiled; for God will judge fornicators and adulterers.* ⁵*Keep your lives free from the love of money, and be content with what you have; for he has said, "I will never leave you or forsake you."* ⁶*So we can say with confidence, "The Lord is my helper; I will not be afraid. What can anyone do to me?"* ⁷*Remember your leaders, those who spoke the word of God to you; consider the outcome of their way of life, and imitate their faith.* ⁸*Jesus Christ is the same yesterday and today and forever.*

The tone and the style of the homily change abruptly in this final chapter. The formal part of the preaching is over, and the speaker now turns to more practical matters of the Christian life.

Yet these exhortations about everyday life in Christ flow directly from what the author has taught about Jesus in the past twelve chapters. The new covenant worship that is acceptable to God includes not just formal adoration and sacramental rituals; it embraces the whole of life. As a priestly people living in Christ, our worship of God in his heavenly sanctuary is rendered through our acts of love on earth. With our enlarged understanding of the priesthood of Christ, we can understand more deeply such earthly realities as hospitality to others, married life, and financial affairs.

"Let mutual love continue" (verse 1) is the foundation of all that follows. Although the word "love" expresses a wide range of meanings in English, the love that our author advocates is a love that is expressed in care for other people, both friends and strangers. Since the sacrifice Jesus offered was an act of total self-giving love and complete solidarity with humanity, our daily offerings, united with his, ought to express that same selfless giving and unity with others.

One of the primary expressions of love for others within the Christian community is the hospitality enjoyed in table fellowship (verse 2). Sharing a meal together creates a bond of love in imitation of the many meals that Jesus shared, both with his disciples and also with strangers and outcasts. Travelers in the ancient world, like those today, needed food, lodging, and a warm welcome along their journey. The allusion to entertaining angels harkens back to the story of Abraham and Sarah as they showed hospitality to the three strangers at Mamre (Gen 18:1–8). Other biblical characters who unknowingly showed hospitality to angels include Gideon (Judg 6:19–22), the parents of Samson (Judg 13:15–16), and Tobit (Tob 5:4ff).

The author then offers advice about caring for those in prison and for victims of torment and abuse (verse 3). While hospitality entails receiving those who come to us, care for prisoners and victims involves going out to meet them to serve their needs. As the preacher was speaking these words, fellow believers were being imprisoned and suffering abuse for their faith. He taught them to assist other Christians with a sense of solidarity and empathy, as if they themselves were in prison and being ill-treated with them. Jesus entered fully into the human condition, so we must serve others as he served.

The next two counsels have to do with disordered desires in two troublesome areas that cause the downfall of many: sex and money. The author urges the community, first, to honor the sanctity of marriage and avoid any sexual activity outside of marriage (verse 4). Second, he tells the congregation to "keep your lives free from the love of money" (verse 5). Like sexual self-indulgence, money promises freedom and then leaves those who chase after it imprisoned. Jesus taught his followers to be radically detached from wealth and possessions. Directing the community away from the drive to continually acquire more, the author quotes two scriptural phrases (Deut 31:6; Ps 118:6) that assure his listeners that God is always with us and will not leave us. Perhaps this suggests that our greed is deeply rooted in a fear of ultimate abandonment. Increased faith leads to confident assurance in the face of whatever adverse circumstances may come our way (verse 6).

After urging his hearers (in chapter 11) to look up to heroes of faith from the ancient past, the author now encourages them to remember those Christian leaders who first brought the word of God to them (verse 7). Because of their holiness, fervor, and fidelity, these founders should be venerated as inspirations and models of faith. The same Jesus Christ preached by those early leaders of the church is alive in the church today (verse 8). He is the same Lord who "yesterday" offered his atoning sacrifice as the new covenant and "today" is enthroned in heaven as God's Son and "forever" intercedes for us in all our needs. His faithfulness is unchanging, so we can have absolute confidence in his promises to us.

Reflection and discussion
- How can an excessive concern for my income and possessions replace the care I must offer to the stranger, the hungry, and the imprisoned?

- What are some ways that I can express solidarity with today's persecuted Christians?

- How can a disordered use of sex and money lead to a kind of imprisonment?

- Why does trusting that God will never leave me or abandon me help me overcome the temptations to greed?

Prayer

Jesus, you are the same yesterday, today, and forever. Thank you for keeping me faithful to my study of Hebrews. May God's word from the past enlighten my life today and guide my path to tomorrow.

LESSON 29 SESSION 6

> **Through him, then, let us continually offer a sacrifice of praise to God, that is, the fruit of lips that confess his name.** HEBREWS 13:15

Offering Sacrifice to God through Christ

HEBREWS 13:9–16 *⁹Do not be carried away by all kinds of strange teachings; for it is well for the heart to be strengthened by grace, not by regulations about food, which have not benefited those who observe them. ¹⁰We have an altar from which those who officiate in the tent have no right to eat. ¹¹For the bodies of those animals whose blood is brought into the sanctuary by the high priest as a sacrifice for sin are burned outside the camp. ¹²Therefore Jesus also suffered outside the city gate in order to sanctify the people by his own blood. ¹³Let us then go to him outside the camp and bear the abuse he endured. ¹⁴For here we have no lasting city, but we are looking for the city that is to come. ¹⁵Through him, then, let us continually offer a sacrifice of praise to God, that is, the fruit of lips that confess his name. ¹⁶Do not neglect to do good and to share what you have, for such sacrifices are pleasing to God.*

Because Jesus Christ is the same yesterday, today, and forever, his followers ought to be wary of deceitful teachings that are incompatible with the gospel. They must make sure they are nourished by God's grace, not by dietary observances and other practices that offer no spiritual benefits (verse 9). For the regulations and rituals of the former covenant have been fulfilled in the once-for-all sacrifice offered by the high priest of the new covenant. We have a new altar, which is the self-offering of Jesus Christ to the Father on our behalf (verse 10). Christians have the privileged "right to eat" at this altar and to partake of its grace. Whereas those who "officiate in the tent" of the covenant of Moses, who have not come to faith in Christ, have no access to this perfected gift.

Once more the author refers to the sin offering of Israel's Day of Atonement to demonstrate its fulfillment in Christ. The sacrificial animals were slaughtered, their blood was shed and brought into the sanctuary, and their bodies were taken to be burned "outside the camp" (verse 11). The contamination of the people's sins was transferred to the animal, and the removal and destruction of the animal eliminated the sin from the community. Yet the body and blood of the animal offered by the high priest were unable to bring about the cleansing from sin and guilt that God desires.

Likewise, in fulfillment of the ancient sin offering, Jesus was brought "outside the city gate" to be crucified, as was typical for public executions (verse 12). His blood was poured out and his body was brutalized, not in the holy temple but in the unholy setting of Golgotha. In fulfillment of the sin offering of the Day of Atonement, Jesus absorbed the guilt of our sins and removed it from us. Thus, he became the perfect sacrifice for sin, the completion of all others, because of the excellence of his offering, the absolute obedience of his will, and the totality of his love.

The ancient covenant considered everything "within the camp" as sacred and everything "outside the camp" as profane. But Jesus reverses the old order and teaches us to follow him with his cross and move outward into the world. Therefore, the preacher exhorts, "let us then go to him outside the camp" (verse 13). The congregation must not take up again the ancient sacrifices of the temple in the city of Jerusalem, the purpose of which has already been accomplished. Rather, they must leave Jerusalem and the sacrificial system of its temple and priesthood, following Jesus and taking on whatever stigma and rejection that entails. For neither Jerusalem nor any other earthly city is lasting because we await the new Jerusalem, "the city that is to come" (verse 14).

Through Jesus Christ, his followers continue to offer sacrifice to God, for indeed Christianity is a sacrificial religion through and through. It is founded on the one, perfect sacrifice of Christ, and the prayers and good works of his church are joined to his sacrifice. The prayers of the community, "the fruit of lips that confess his name," become "a sacrifice of praise to God" (verse 15). The community's good works—sharing what they have, obeying their leaders, showing hospitality to strangers, caring for prisoners—become sacrifices "pleasing to God" (verse 16).

This worship of God in the new covenant is the once-for-all sacrifice of the Son united with all the prayers, works, joys, and sufferings of his church. The many sacrifices offered in Jerusalem's temple accomplished their purpose as they pointed to the self-offering of Christ. Hebrews has demonstrated that our worship is rooted in our understanding of what God has accomplished for us in his Son. The pattern of priestly mediation for acceptable sacrifice, established under the law of Moses, has now come to its perfect completion in Christ, as Hebrews has explained. What is pleasing to God is a life of mutual love, grateful obedience, faithful commitment, and humble generosity that is offered through, with, and in Jesus Christ, the high priest and mediator of our worship.

Reflection and discussion

- New covenant worship has both a vertical dimension, oriented to God, and a horizontal dimension, oriented toward our neighbors. What are some examples of each?

- In what ways is my Christian life fueled and nourished from the new covenant altar of Christ's sacrifice?

- Why must we seek Christ "outside the camp"?

- In what sense is Christianity a thoroughly sacrificial religion?

Prayer

Loving Father, I offer you my prayers, works, joys, and sufferings of this day, in union with the eternal sacrifice of your Son, Jesus. May my life be, in your eyes, an acceptable sacrifice of praise.

LESSON 30 **SESSION 6**

> I appeal to you, brothers and sisters, bear with my word
> of exhortation, for I have written to you briefly.
> HEBREWS 13:22

Final Blessing and Postscript

HEBREWS 13:17–25 ¹⁷*Obey your leaders and submit to them, for they are keeping watch over your souls and will give an account. Let them do this with joy and not with sighing—for that would be harmful to you.*

¹⁸Pray for us; we are sure that we have a clear conscience, desiring to act honorably in all things. ¹⁹I urge you all the more to do this, so that I may be restored to you very soon.

²⁰Now may the God of peace, who brought back from the dead our Lord Jesus, the great shepherd of the sheep, by the blood of the eternal covenant, ²¹make you complete in everything good so that you may do his will, working among us that which is pleasing in his sight, through Jesus Christ, to whom be the glory forever and ever. Amen.

²²I appeal to you, brothers and sisters, bear with my word of exhortation, for I have written to you briefly. ²³I want you to know that our brother Timothy has been set free; and if he comes in time, he will be with me when I see you. ²⁴Greet all your leaders and all the saints. Those from Italy send you greetings. ²⁵Grace be with all of you.

Hebrews ends with a closing exhortation, final blessing, and postscript. The conclusion offers us enticing morsels of information concerning the author and his listeners. Yet the origins, context, and setting of this biblical book remain a mystery. Despite its beautiful style and rich theology, we still don't know who wrote it, where it was written, to whom it was written, or when it was written.

The author urges his hearers to obey their leaders and submit to their authority (verse 17). Just as the law of Moses offered a leadership structure, so the new covenant provides leaders with pastoral authority over God's people. They are responsible for watching over the souls entrusted to them. These leaders are the successors of those who first brought the gospel to this community and formed the local church. The congregation is urged to see that their leaders fulfill their ministry "with joy and not with sighing," for the church flourishes when there is mutual respect, trust, and collaboration among all the members.

The close relationship between the author and the congregation is evident as he requests their prayers and expresses his desire to return to them soon (verses 18–19). Clearly he holds them in great affection although he is some distance away from them. His assurances of a clear conscience and the desire to act honorably in all things could suggest that he has been involved in some controversy and been detained because of it. However, it could just as well be accentuating that his homily, despite its stern admonitions, is free of self-interest and motivated only by his pastoral concern.

The final blessing is a beautiful conclusion to this remarkable homily, tying together many of the themes that the author has developed (verses 20–21). It invokes the "God of peace," referring to peace in the biblical sense of the Hebrew "shalom," meaning wholeness and completeness. God has established peace between himself and humanity by the sacrifice of his Son. He is also the one who "brought back from the dead our Lord Jesus." The resurrection is the completion and perfection of Christ's sacrifice, enabling us to live in him and offer our lives in union with him. As "the great shepherd of the sheep," Jesus cares for his church and lays down his life for his people. As the great shepherd, he loves his people to the end, and as the great high priest, he gives his life in sacrifice for them.

"Through Jesus Christ," the transitory reality of the former covenant has given way to the "eternal covenant." Through the blood of his perfect sacrifice and through his resurrection, God equips us with every good thing so that we do his will, and God works within us so that our lives may be pleasing in his sight. So all of our loving deeds, our hope in the future, our acts of faithfulness and courage, our struggles and suffering—all of these are now signs that God is at work within us and among us through the grace of the new covenant.

The final verses are a postscript added to the homily when it was sent to the community (verses 22–25). Here the author defines Hebrews as "my word of exhortation"—an apt description of what we have read—and says he has written "briefly," suggesting that he may elaborate these teachings at greater length when the occasion presents itself. He informs the community that Timothy, a well-known and gifted missionary in the early church, has been released and may visit them soon. Finally, he greets the leaders of the church and all its members, "the saints," and sends greeting from "those from Italy." It is impossible to say, however, whether the author is in Italy writing to another location or writing to Italy from another location where some Italian Christians are now residing.

Despite these few indicators of person and place, the origins of Hebrews remain a mystery. What is no longer a mystery, however, is the message of Hebrews. This magnificent book of the New Testament now provides us with a deeper understanding of Jesus and the meaning of his life for us.

Reflection and discussion
- Why is it important to pray for the pastoral leaders of the church?

- What is the primary insight I have gained from studying Hebrews?

- After studying Hebrews, what seems to be the most distinctive characteristic of new covenant worship?

- Slowly reading again the blessing in verses 20–21, what do I desire God to complete in me?

Prayer

God of peace, through my reflection on your inspired word in Hebrews, work within my mind and heart so that I can live my life in greater union with your Son, and so become a pleasing offering to you.

SUGGESTIONS FOR FACILITATORS, GROUP SESSION 6

1. Welcome group members and make any final announcements or requests.

2. You may want to pray this prayer as a group:
   God of Sinai and Zion, of the ancient covenant with Israel and the new covenant in Jesus, we are grateful for the ways you have guided your people in every age, leading them to deeper experiences of your divine mercy. Through our reflection on your inspired word in Hebrews, work within our minds and hearts so that we may live in greater union with your Son, and so become a pleasing sacrifice of praise.

3. Ask one or more of the following questions:
   - How has this study of Hebrews enriched your life?
   - In what way has this study challenged you the most?

4. Discuss lessons 25 through 30. Choose one or more of the questions for reflection and discussion from each lesson to discuss as a group.

5. Ask the group if they would like to study another in the *Threshold Bible Study* series. Discuss the topic and dates, and make a decision among those interested. Ask the group members to suggest people they would like to invite to participate in the next study series.

6. Ask the group to discuss the insights that stand out most from this study over the past six weeks.

7. Conclude by praying aloud the following prayer or another of your own choosing:
   Holy Spirit of the living God, you inspired the writers of the Scriptures and you have guided our study during these weeks. Continue to deepen our love for the word of God in the holy Scriptures and draw us more deeply into the heart of Jesus. We thank you for the confident hope you have placed within us and the gifts that build up the church. Through this study, lead us to worship and witness more fully and fervently, and bless us now and always with the fire of your love.

Ordering Additional Studies

AVAILABLE TITLES IN THIS SERIES INCLUDE…

- Advent Light
- Angels of God
- Divine Mercy
- Eucharist
- The Feasts of Judaism
- Forgiveness
- God's Spousal Love
- The Holy Spirit and Spiritual Gifts
- Jerusalem, the Holy City
- Missionary Discipleship
- Mysteries of the Rosary
- The Names of Jesus
- Peacemaking and Nonviolence
- People of the Passion
- Pilgrimage in the Footsteps of Jesus
- Questions Jesus Asks
- The Resurrection and the Life
- The Sacred Heart of Jesus
- Stewardship of the Earth
- The Tragic and Triumphant Cross
- Wholehearted Commitment
  PART 1: Deuteronomy 1–15
  PART 2: Deuteronomy 16–34
- Jesus, the Messianic King
  PART 1: Matthew 1–16
  PART 2: Matthew 17–28
- Jesus, the Suffering Servant
  PART 1: Mark 1–8
  PART 2: Mark 9–16
- Jesus, the Compassionate Savior
  PART 1: Luke 1–11
  PART 2: Luke 12–24
- Jesus, the Word Made Flesh
  PART 1: John 1–10
  PART 2: John 11–21
- Church of the Holy Spirit
  PART 1: Acts of the Apostles 1–14
  PART 2: Acts of the Apostles 15–28
- Salvation Offered for All People:
  Romans
- Proclaiming Christ Crucified:
  1 Corinthians
- The Lamb and the Beasts:
  The Book of Revelation

TO CHECK AVAILABILITY OR FOR A DESCRIPTION
OF EACH STUDY, VISIT OUR WEBSITE AT
www.ThresholdBibleStudy.com
OR CALL US AT **1-800-321-0411**